THE FUR-LINED MOUSETRAP

THE
FUR-LINED MOUSETRAP

C. Northcote Parkinson

Text illustrations by michael ffolkes

LEVIATHAN HOUSE LTD
LONDON & NEW YORK

ISBN 0 900537 05 1

PRINTED IN GREAT BRITAIN
BY W & J MACKAY LIMITED, CHATHAM

Contents

Preface

The great debate in Britain over the last decade and more has centred upon the possibility of Britain entering the European Economic Community. There have been tense moments in Parliament and the newspapers have printed columns of information and comment upon the results which might follow Britain's entry; the results more especially as affecting employment, currency, agricultural subsidies and the balance of trade. But the problem is a political one and its economic consequences are not of comparable importance. Is there to be a United States of Europe and is Britain to form a part of it? That is the biggest question we in Twentieth Century Britain will ever have to answer. It is not my purpose here to promote or oppose the cause of European unity but merely to comment on the way in which this vital issue has been discussed. What have our leading authors had to say on the subject? What guidance have we had from our more distinguished writers, dramatists and poets?

Fifty years ago no great decision was ever taken before our leading authors had said their say. The newspapers of that period gave a wide circulation to the views expressed by George Bernard Shaw, by H. G. Wells, by Dean Inge and Arnold Bennett. It would be difficult to measure what influence they had for their views, when opposed, would tend to cancel out. What their writings did ensure was that the case on either side would be cogently presented in a literary form. Powerful intellects were brought to bear on every public issue and the merest schoolboy would be jolted into awareness of the arguments put forward. Nor could we always guess in advance what an original thinker would have to say. Would G. B. Shaw be opposed to capital punishment? He was for it and argued for its wider use. Was H. G. Wells a pacifist? He was, in fact, the inventor of a war game to be played with model soldiers. What had Galsworthy to say about justice? What were G. K. Chesterton's views on the Boer War? There was a time when neither politicians nor public could ignore what thinkers had to say. Times are altered now and the influential author has simply vanished from the scene.

To illustrate this point let us suppose that Rudyard Kipling and Hilaire Belloc were still alive and active; two great journalists, two poets of distinction, two known masters of the written word. In the issue before us, that of Britain's entry into a potentially united Europe, we have a debate which would suit them both. On the one side we should have the prophet of Empire; on the other, the author of *The Path to Rome*. Here would be the impact of the irresistible force on the immovable obstacle—a battle of the giants. Belloc would point to the historic unity of Christendom, to the spirit of the crusades, to the story of the marching legions and the legends which haunt the pass of Roncevalles. He would appeal to the tradition of two thousand years, recalling that 'Hope of the half defeated, shrine of gold, sword of the Faith and Tower of Ivory'. But what ivory tower could resist Rudyard Kipling, whose God of Hosts was with him yet, Lord of the farflung battle line? He would stir us afresh with talk of the Empire, that magic brotherhood of peoples, sundered from each other by the oceans, joined in mystic homage to the Queen. He would lead us in spirit from the ramparts of Quebec to the barracks at Rawalpindi, from the advancing bayonets at Ladysmith to the surf which thunders on the West Australian shore. He would show us the folly of looking back on Europe, urging us rather to look onwards and outwards, dwelling rather on our dominion over palm and pine. Kipling and Belloc were contemporaries, remember, each with a pen, paper, print and a point of view.

What have the authors of today to offer us by way of inspiration and counsel? What modern Kipling is there to plead the cause of the Commonwealth, showing us what life may linger yet in that noble concept? What modern Belloc have we to point the way to a united Europe in which the Faith may yet triumph over heresy and disunion over corruption and decay? In which of our contemporaries can we see a Dickens, a Trollope, a Reade or an H. G. Wells? What has present-day London to offer us? We have had dramatists with their heads in the kitchen sink, if not in the gas-oven. There are young authors who look back in anger, their indignation sometimes outlasting their youth. There are the highbrow poets and the lowbrow comedians. There are the sociologists, the economists and calculators. All that we lack is the magic of authorship, the wisdom that used to find its way into print and the space found in the press for such wisdom as there was. It is possible, though far from certain, that some current authors, if offered any public encouragement, might have something of interest to say. To illustrate this point, I have collected here some of the thoughts I have had the chance to express, some from the platform and some in print. A number of these are essays in business administration but some range more widely and not all are written with the same degree of solemnity. My master, as an essayist, was the late Mr. G. K. Chesterton, whose equal I could never claim to be. I should be proud, however, if any writing of mine had tended to keep alive the author's freedom to comment on the issues of the day.

Some of the views put forward in this preface were first expressed in a speech to the Paternosters. Chapter 2 was first printed as a contribution to the magazine *Incentive* in 1969. The gist of Chapter 3 was delivered to a conference held at the Villa d'Este, Lake Como, under the auspices of the Management Institute of Europe. In Chapter 4, I repeat the message I gave to the Association of Swiss Industrial Engineers, held at Lucerne in 1969. Chapter 5 is based upon a lecture given to Danish advertising agents at Copenhagen. Peter's Predicament has appeared in *The Los Angeles Times*, and Chapter 8 in the *Sunday Times* of 5 July, 1970. 'Left is Right' appeared with a slightly different title in *Saturday Evening Post* and 'Revolting Youth' (Chapter 10) is based upon a lecture delivered at Heidelberg under arrangements made by the Gesellschaft für Industrielle Schulung. Chapter 11 includes material from a lecture I gave to the Teachers Training College at Leeds and much of Chapter 12 derives from a Commencement Address delivered at a Convocation of the University of Illinois. I am beholden to editors and sponsors for permission to reprint in book form all that has previously been published. I have a still greater debt, however, to those who have helped me with the publication of this book; notably Dr. George Copeman for his editorial advice and Mrs. K. Green for her patience in translating my illegible handwriting into typescript. To Ann, I am indebted for her help and encouragement over the last twenty years, without which nothing I have done would have been worth the effort.

C. Northcote Parkinson

CHAPTER 1

The Fur-lined Mousetrap

Three mice were studying a structure of steel wires erected on an oblong wooden base. From inside this strange piece of equipment came the tempting smell of cheese. On its carpeted floor lay an expensive-looking fur and the steel tent was itself apparently lined with the same costly material. From the standpoint of the mice, as they inspected it, the open entrance to this paradise was on their left and marked by a simple signpost. The word MICE was the only inscription, enough in itself to make the invitation clear. As the mice hesitated, the senior of them, whose coat was a conservative dark grey, thought it his duty to advise his two companions. He opened the discussion on a note of warning.

'As the oldest among you I feel bound to give you the benefit of my experience. Years ago I was confronted by a structure similar to this—not identical, I'll admit, but with some points of resemblance—and I wondered then, as I do now, whether what seemed to be a generous offer might not include some unforeseen drawback. While I was still considering this possibility a contemporary of mine pushed me aside—rather rudely as I thought at the time—and approached the cheese, which appeared to be a cheddar of good quality. As he did so the floor sank slightly beneath his weight and a steel wire flashed down. He was killed instantly, poor mouse, and it was I who had the painful task of informing his widow. I must not conceal from you my suspicion that this may be a contrivance of the same pattern, the work of racists who practice genocide. I would advise you, my friends, to leave it alone.'

Second to speak was a white mouse with red eyes who thanked the grey mouse for his advice but begged to differ from him. 'Speaking as a mouse with some technical knowledge,' he said, 'I question whether the structure before us can resemble the one which proved so fatal to your companion. Where is the steel wire which could fall on us? I see nothing which has more than a super-ficial resemblance to the device you have described.'

The third mouse was pink in colour, excitable in manner and emphatic in his views.

'What you have just said, comrade,' he cried, 'is no more than the truth. I should myself describe this piece of furniture as func-tional and even modernistic; not to the taste, perhaps, of the elderly. Prejudice apart, however, the design is successful. More than that, the fur-lining appears to be mink—or, anyway, mus-quash—and my guess is that the cheese is stilton or, possibly, camembert. Forward, comrades, to the mouse millennium!'

On hearing this eloquent plea, the three mice advanced with confidence and circled to the left, entering the box that had been planned for them. They tasted the cheese, which turned out to be a processed variety from the Co-operative Stores. They lay down on the fur—a very creditable imitation—and said to each other, 'This is the life!' As they said these words, however, the cage door fell with an ominous click. The trap had closed and they were inside it.

Mice are useful to the scientist but they are not among the more intelligent animals, even the most astute of them being intellectually inferior to man. We should be surprised, therefore, if we were to hear of mankind falling readily into the sort of trap which ensnared the mice. Human beings, we feel, are too sophisticated for that. That is not to say, however, that they would not fall into another sort of trap, one which would attract them in a more complex way and imprison them by less obvious means. If such a trap should exist today its framework would consist of economic realities and it would be baited with the promise of social security. A very little reflection must lead us, moreover, to the conclusion that such a trap is among those already on the market. To understand its mechanism we need to have looked at the earlier chapters of some economic textbook and such is the world of today that few of us can claim to have escaped this experience. We are bombarded, moreover, with further information in every party political broadcast. We have been pursued with daily doses of the dismal science, our politicians having little to say, in fact, on any other topic. We have been exposed since childhood to the explanation of economic principles. One of the more plausible of them concerns the expected alternation of boom and slump. Economists may not agree on the cause of this phenomenon but we know by now what is supposed to happen, and the more elderly among us have even witnessed it. We could describe the whole process in harrowing detail. It begins with a loss of confidence on the stock exchange where the sellers are many and the buyers are few. Prices fall but potential investors are still reluctant, convinced as they are that the fall will continue. Some speculators are ruined at this point, returning home white-faced to confess to their wives that they have lost everything. There follows a drop in the price of goods and services, all sorts of commodities being marked down. With sales declining and the margin of profit reduced, manufacturers curtail their output and discharge their less valuable employees. Some firms go out of business and there is a corresponding rise in the numbers of the unemployed. This again reduces the demand for goods and hence the output, putting more employers out of business and adding again to the numbers of the unemployed. The country has entered a phase of economic depression, one that may extend to other countries or indeed to all.

Surveying this unhappy scene, the good businessman does not merely express his grief. He knows that the secret of success in speculation or investment is simple and indeed obvious. He must buy when everyone else is selling and sell when everyone else is buying. Nothing could be more plainly a matter of common sense. The practice is, however, a little more difficult than the theory and especially so during a trade depression. For to buy when others are selling implies, first of all, that you have the money and the courage and second, that the price is not going to fall again. The future millionaire is therefore the man who foresaw the slump and sold out, putting his money into a deposit account. The future multi-millionaire is the man who did that and who then senses the moment when prices are as low as they are likely to go. Buying at that moment he waits patiently until better times, believing as he does that each slump must be followed by a boom. When he sells it will be at the moment when everyone else is buying.

All this is the commonplace of the textbook. It is no longer, however, a description of what actually takes place. For the politicians and civil servants, having also studied the textbook, are resolved to prevent the depression which they see as a threat to their respective votes and salaries. The trade union officials, having read the same textbook, are resolved that union members shall not have to face a fall in the level of their wages. There is thus a general belief that the danger can be averted by governmental activity. The wage level is maintained (or raised) and the accepted policy is to create employment. This can be done by printing more paper money, by lending capital to the less successful manufacturers, by coming to the rescue of tottering industries, and by spending lavishly in what is called the public sector of the economy. Obsolete factories are coaxed into prolonging their existence in dying areas of past enterprise. Bankrupt companies are given more money to lose and local authorities are urged to widen their roads and enlarge their schools. People who would otherwise be unemployed are kept in class, recruited as civil servants or sent to college. The crisis is more or less averted and we are faced at the time of writing by a situation which the classical economists had no occasion to describe; a period of rising wages and prices accompanied by a high rate of unemployment. We have thus the symptoms without the results of a trade depression. The inflation which undermined the pensioner during the boom is prolonged so as to complete his destruction during the slump. Wages are held at a high average and strikes are staged so as to push them higher. All the accepted rules have been broken and even the unemployed are paid more than other less fortunate people are paid for working. The situation is utopian and is certainly conducive to the greatest happiness of the greatest number. For some people (not all) there is, it would seem, a fur-lined future.

It is fair to ask at this point whether our economic problem has been solved? Have we in fact built Jerusalem in England's mean unpleasant land? Our experience of life has tended to prove that everything has its price. We have therefore the uneasy feeling that present comfort must have been purchased at the expense of something else. So far as Britain is concerned, what has obviously gone is, of course, our currency, once the most stable (and most sensible) coinage in the world. We have accepted in its place a load of rubbish which will soon, no doubt, be valueless. But is that all? Is there no other drawback, no other item on the debit side? There is one item in which we might reasonably show a pensive interest and that is our society's capacity for righting itself. The modern lifeboat is so designed that it will recover after capsizing. Following even the most gigantic sea the lifeboat is supposed to reappear once more with its wheelhouse uppermost and its keel invisible. The same could once be said of an industrial society hit by a depression. But it is true of the society we have? To change the metaphor, it would be easy to design a mousetrap in which a mouse might be extremely comfortable. It could have every convenience from tufted carpet to central heating. It could have Mickey Mouse programmes on its closed circuit television set. It might be available in a de luxe model actually lined with fur. For the mouse concerned the sole drawback would lie in the lack of exit. Fur-lined or not, the device would still be a trap.

What used to happen? How did the slump end in the bad old

days when the slump was not prevented? We have seen that the wise investor would bide his time but why could he be sure that things would improve? In times gone by the point would be reached when goods were cheap, when wages were low and when wits were sharpened by bleak necessity. Wealth is the foe of ingenuity, causing people to rely upon money instead of brains. Hard times provide scope for intellect, creating the situation in which a new enterprise may be launched with maximum effort but at minimal cost. As one business after another is revived or founded, each on a shoestring, the recession gradually comes to an end. Despondency gives way to hope and that is in turn replaced by confidence. Business improves under conditions which make for success. Scores of bankruptcies have cleared away the rubbish, the deadwood has been swept aside and those still in the forefront are men whose ability has been proved. As from this time a happier period begins but its prosperity is based upon previous hardship but for which the scene would still be cumbered by all that is obsolete and hidebound. The slump has served its purpose and the foundations of a new prosperity are built upon the ruins. The boom—like the slump—will not last for ever but we older people would mostly agree that the alternation is necessary to business. In a healthily competitive market, neither the sellers nor the buyers should have it eternally their own way.

This is a fair picture, surely, of what used to happen. Things are different now and there are many who welcome the change, arguing that we have done away with past miseries. No one starves, few are significantly poorer and even the married men who go on strike are maintained, in effect, out of public funds. We thus live in a more comfortable world than our ancestors ever knew. We are cushioned, moreover, against the hardships and worries to which many other peoples are still exposed. But we may still be in a trap from which there is no escape. For the factors are absent which used to save us. There has been no drastic elimination of useless firms and incompetent individuals. Our industrial landscape is still littered with useless debris from past periods of enterprise. Equipment is still in use which ought to be on the scrapheap or in a museum. People are still employed who should have been discharged. Capital is still tied up in moribund factories and dying trades. Wages are high enough to deter us from expanding our work force. There is nothing in the situation to encourage anyone to do anything. In terms of mere business our society would seem to be in a cul-de-sac. There is a measure of comfort and a minimum of risk but we may be wondering whether we are really in the promised land. The fur, for example, was never more than an imitation and now seems to be wearing thin. As for the cheese, it tastes mostly of tinfoil and is no longer even plentiful. What remain unaltered are the cage we entered and the cage door which cannot be opened from the inside. We may be comfortable but the trap has closed and we are in it.

We may be comfortable but the trap has closed and we are in it

CHAPTER 2

Incentives and Penalties

'And when the woman saw that the tree was good for food and that it was pleasant to the eyes, and a tree to be desired to make one wise, she took of the fruit thereof, and did eat, and gave also to her husband with her; and he did eat. And the eyes of them both were opened, and they knew that they were naked. . . .' When they had eaten the forbidden fruit Adam and Eve were expelled from Eden, not to deprive them of knowledge (for in that respect the damage had been done) but to prevent them finding the tree of life, the fruit of which would have given them infinite longevity. Not being expressly told to leave that tree alone, they had evidently not even noticed it. They emerged from Eden, therefore, with mortality as a family characteristic. They had also acquired a pattern of incentives which has since been improved in only one respect. They had been tempted into disobedience by the prospect of (a) food (and shelter), (b) beauty, (c) knowledge, (d) sex, and (e) misconduct. A prospect of the same rewards might have lured them into any other course of action, with murder a possibility and work not wholly inconceivable. Going to the root of the matter, the author of the Book of Genesis has thus listed the considerations which will arouse the average human being into possibly unwonted activity. These, with one added, are the basic incentives.

It was remarked once in Malaya that the average Englishman, coming to the tropics for his livelihood, has always before him the prospect of retirement. When pressed to explain what retirement will mean to him he will describe a place in the country with decent scenery and climate, some rough shooting and fishing, a garden and some congenial neighbours, an occasional day in town and leisure in which to take his dog for a walk. With this distant prospect as incentive, many a European has worked for a lifetime and died, in fact, at his post overseas. For the whole of that time he will have noted, often with disapproval, the apparent idleness of the Malay. A moderately primitive people, the Malays usually reject the more arduous forms of work, preferring to be employed as politicians, soldiers, policemen or chauffeurs. The planter or merchant will sometimes sadly contrast their inactivity with the more hard-working life of the Chinese or Indian. What he may not always realize is that the Malay, with tastes not unlike his own, has had from birth all the conditions for retirement which the Englishman is working to achieve. He was born in the country with a decent climate, river scenery, a pleasant existence and enough to eat. He lacks the incentive to over-work and needs money only perhaps for cigarettes or the cinema. To own a bicycle, he thinks, may be good but to sit in the shade (he concludes) may be better.

The author of Genesis describes the basic human incentives with accuracy, not omitting to add the lure of what is deemed to be naughty. In only one respect does he fall short of the universal and that is in equating nakedness with sex. A Greek would thus have associated nakedness more with athletics. We might add that ideas of naughtiness are variable, the illicit being attractive but not uniform. Now the post-Genesis advance of civilization introduced one other major incentive at a very early period. This was the incentive of Status, which assumes significance from the moment that the other human needs are even partially met. Such, moreover, is its importance that it soon colours our attitude towards food, beauty, knowledge, sex and naughtiness. Status is of two kinds, based respectively upon authority and wealth. We do not exclude a combination of the two but the two ideas remain distinct, the

D.S.O. and the Rolls Royce being symbols of status in a different way. In countries with an aristocratic tradition (like Britain) the highest status is associated with official position, birth, education, athletic prowess and gallantry in battle. In countries without any such tradition (like U.S.A.) the highest status is associated with the biggest capital and income. Very seldom do we meet a millionaire with the V.C., and Sir Thomas More's achievement, in being both knighted and canonized, is likely to remain an unbeaten record.

As already hinted, the concept of Status comes to colour the older and more basic incentives. Food of the status-seeker is caviare and champagne. Beauty is provided by the mansion or penthouse, and knowledge by the chatter of those who are unusually well-informed. Sex has to be sophisticated and naughtiness should be of a kind that humbler folk could not even have imagined. There might in theory be folk who lack incentive because they already have everything, and such people may even exist in fact. They are rare, however, because the person with wealth may be longing for authority and the person with authority may be lacking in wealth. John F. Kennedy's magic derived from having both with a record, besides, of active service. There are few men in that category, the rest of us having more pressing incentives at far lower levels. And society owes its dynamic energy to the efforts we make in achieving our several ambitions. The total energy available is the sum of our efforts and it is directly proportional to the difference in authority or wealth between the highest and lowest levels of society. Our efforts to equalize status have the effect of reducing the total energy and were they wholly successful (which they never are) the sum of our energies would be reduced to NIL.

There are theorists who tell us that the citizens of an ideal society would require no incentive. Properly motivated, they would work and think and invent for the good of the community and the benefit of mankind. Other theorists tell us, quite wrongly, that such a society cannot survive. In point of fact such selfless communities exist today and have existed for centuries. They are the world's monasteries, Buddhist and Christian, and no one can say that they have been unproductive. The condition which governs their success, however, is the exclusion of sex. In the Garden of Eden the first person to react to an incentive (apart from the serpent) was Eve. It was *she* who made the original effort and she had both a mini-skirt and a mink before they first came to move house. Symbolically at least, this has always been the fact. Left to himself, a monk may be content with a state of contemplation. Give him a wife and she wants to see some proof of his affection. Give him children and he wants to see them clothed, fed and taught in an expensive way. The motive force is not provided by human selfishness but by human love. So far is this from being a motive of which we need be ashamed that we are justified, more probably, in doubting whether society could be organized in any other way. There are monasteries, to be sure, but a world entirely monastic would soon come to an untimely end.

It is usual to depict a stratified society as a pyramid up which people try to scramble, but it is possible to change the simile and regard people as mostly born on the barren mountain side, from which they strive to gain the comfort of the fertile valley. In their efforts to descend they drive the water-wheels and dynamos which give society its motive force. Without incentives they would remain and stagnate at the higher levels. Given incentive enough and opportunity sufficient they will find their way down and do useful work in the process. But much depends upon the nature of the channels through which their energies flow. If these are narrow yet feasible, demanding effort but with promise of eventual success, the maximum of power will generate for the benefit of all. Widen the channels too much and the motive power will die away for lack of concentration. Narrow them too much, presenting a seemingly complete obstacle, and all is brought to a standstill, with the likelihood of an eventual burst and overflow. In a dynamic society the art of government involves the regulation of the channels for ambition. Only by the finest adjustment will they gain the best results. Too many existing societies present the picture of an elaborate machine without motive power, and these are the societies we describe as 'permissive'. They have permitted the escape of the forces they might have used.

Once the basic needs have been met, the human desire is for status, as we have seen, and this rests upon either authority or wealth. And the British preference is for authority. We thus reserve our highest admiration for admirals and generals, for cricket players and actresses, for mountaineers who have climbed Everest, for yachtsmen who have rounded the Horn. The respect we have for the airline pilot is not increased by our knowledge that he is highly paid. Our system, moreover, of rewarding merit can easily make a poor man more than the equal of the wealthiest neighbour. We have been taught to look with some suspicion on wealth, refusing to see in it any proof of merit. Should a fortune be inherited, we think the heir merely lucky and probably worthless. Should it be earned by honest enterprise, we hint that the owner must have been selfish, ruthless and mean. It is arguable, however, that moneymaking is often more innocent than is generally believed. What is still more to the point is our belated realization that little of beauty is ever created without the existence of someone to pay for it.

We have treated of incentives at the highest level, whether of finance or mountain climbing, but the same reasoning applies to folk whose aspirations fall short of the summit. There is nothing more natural than a man's desire to provide his family with a house of their own, detached if he can afford it and provided with garage, garden and paddle pool. There is nothing more reasonable than his wish to give his children a better education than he himself received, with holidays abroad and the chance perhaps to ski and sail. All these opportunities are admittedly the symbols of status but who will work overtime if there is no status to be bought? Who otherwise will study at night to gain some extra qualification? The man who concludes that nothing is too good for the girl he has married, is a better human being than the fanatic who thinks only of a marxist future in which his neighbours will be liquidated as heretics. There may be nothing particularly noble about making money but there are ambitions which may prove infinitely worse. The craving for power is less admirable, as a rule, than the craving for comfort. There is nothing more depressing in this respect than the communist city in which there is nothing to buy. The necessities of life are there—the fuel, the food and the clothing—but additional earning is futile for there is little more to be had. It is only when incentives have gone that we realize fully what their value used to be.

Converse of the incentive is the disincentive, the use of the stick as contrasted with the offer of the carrot. Modern sensibilities must almost prevent us from discussing the value of disincentives but it would be dishonest to end the discussion without some passing reference to their application. The original disincentive is described in *Genesis*. 'Of every tree of the garden thou mayest freely eat: but of the tree of the knowledge of good and evil, thou shalt not eat of it; for in the day that thou eatest thereof *thou shalt surely die.*' This would seem to make the situation fairly clear but the pre-scribed penalty was not enforced, Adam living (we are told) for 930 years. Even the serpent got off lightly but Adam's descendants, with the exception of Noah, mostly paid the death penalty for crimes which are not exactly recorded. Rather more precisely indicated are the offences which brought destruction upon Sodom and Gomorrah. There is altogether no lack in *Genesis* of retribution for failure to obey the Lord. It would not seem, however, that the examples made had much effect. We are thus driven to the con-clusion that the direct incentive is more effective than the dis-incentive, the carrot more useful than the stick. A possible explana-tion of this fact might be based on the theory that the wrong donkey is beaten every time.

The man who concludes that nothing is too good for the girl he has married. . . .

CHAPTER 3

Government and Business

There is a traditional conflict—as seen particularly in U.S.A.—between private enterprise and governmental control. National governments, as seen by business men, are obstructive, incompetent, out-of-date, corrupt and slow. Industrial groups, as seen by the civil servants, are selfish, ruthless, unpatriotic, anti-social and mean. In their own eyes, the bureaucrats are high-minded, selfless, dedicated, hard-working and highly intelligent. In their own eyes, business men are energetic, daring, far-sighted, generous to a fault and known above all for their integrity. We may doubt whether either group is as virtuous and noble as seen by itself or as despicable as seen by the other. They are probably more similar, in fact, than anyone on either side would care to admit. They also depend upon each other more than they always realize or remember. There are differences, however, and we need to list them before we attempt to resolve, or even describe, the conflict which must result from their opposition and contrast.

There are three basic differences and the first of these is immediately obvious. A government, composed of politicians and civil servants, works within a national boundary. Its interests and activities stop abruptly at the frontier. That is why there seems to be no solution for a problem, like that of oil pollution at sea, which arises beyond territorial waters. Business men may have frontiers of their own and cannot, in any case, ignore the political boundaries, but their activities are within an industry or a group of industries, their market is a world market and their capital may be drawn from countries other than their own. In the world of today our efforts to form a world government are bound to fail for just as long as we entrust its organization to politicians rather than to people who are already thinking of the world as one. Shell executives may live in a country of their own but the company extends over the whole world and is so integrated that its citizens hardly notice, round the boardroom table, whether any director is British or Dutch by origin. If the world is to survive at all, there is an urgent need for people who can see the problem as a whole. These include mathematicians, scientists, athletes, chess-players, acrobats, bankers, ballet dancers and oil executives. Politicians are expressly ruled out and all the more finally if they should happen to have been elected by some democratic process, for they are, in that event, tied down by their mere terms of reference. When elected, they represent the interests of their constituents. They may come in time to represent the interests of their country. They were not elected to save the world, however, and they would lose the next election if they expressed any concern about it. The democratic politician is parochial in his outlook and must so remain if he is to stay in office.

The second basic difference between government and business lies in their respective attitudes towards finance. The success or failure of a business is to be understood from the figures shown in a balance sheet. The success or failure of a government cannot be measured by any purely mathematical process and is difficult, in fact, to measure at all. Nor is there any method of assessment upon which the world is agreed. The present author has put forward one method but without gaining world approval as yet, and it is far from certain whether governments even *want* to be assessed. In the meanwhile the contrast remains, especially in matters of finance. A business is judged in terms of profit and loss. A government failure is only apparent when there is a revolution. In theory we could ask whether people are content with a certain government or even with a certain form of rule. But what is the answer to be? Some are, some are not, and the majority have not even thought about it. In general, then, we can claim that business is more competent than government and could hardly survive if it were not.

The third basic difference arises from the fact that what government is attempting to do is far more complex than anything we attempt to achieve as business men. We who are in business should remember this before we become too complacent about our relative efficiency. Leaders of industry are people in a position to lose money: that is their essential characteristic. That is what distinguishes them from soldiers, seamen, policemen and clergy. Soldiers may fail to gain promotion. Policemen may even face dismissal and disgrace. Running those same risks, industrialists face, in addition, the actual loss of money they have invested, together with the loss of possibly larger sums which have been entrusted to them by other people. This is a heavy responsibility, one which affects their wives and families, their ancestors and descendants, their colleagues, their associates, their employees and friends. Any error they make can bring disaster to thousands. Any success, on the other hand, may bring prosperity to the same people as would suffer if they failed. That is the burden they have to bear, their hopes and fears being proportionate to the sums invested. But having conceded so much, we must still insist that the industrialist's task is at least relatively simple. He wants to manufacture what people will want to buy. He wants to sell things at a higher price than he has paid for them. He wants to show a trading profit.

For the politician or civil servant the task is infinitely more complex. He has to apply human energies and revenue to such diverse purposes as security, law and order, health, education, welfare, research, conservation and the balance of trade. When the international consortium wants to drill for oil in the national park, when the factory effluent pollutes the river, it falls to the politician or bureaucrat to say 'No'. There is no one else in a position to prevent the damage or, for that matter, to strike a balance between the advantages and drawbacks. When it comes to the siting of a new airport, we are all agreed that it is essential and we all want it somewhere else. It falls to the government to make a decision in terms of communication, convenience, amenities and cost. Were it a business decision the answer would be relatively simple and subject to arithmetical proof. It is, however, a political decision with factors in the situation which include the measurement of noise, the provision of employment, the strength of local agitation, the antiquity of a given church and the preservation of wildfowl on a certain lake.

To those who are building a high rise building the worst disaster is to find a Roman temple beneath the topsoil, thus creating a new situation in which all sorts of other considerations confuse the issue. But that is not an everyday situation. In the course of ordinary transactions it is the essence of business to isolate the economic motive and make that the prime and often the only consideration which affects the decision. It is the essence of politics, by contrast, to blend a whole range of considerations—military, financial, religious, social, aesthetic—and give only the proper weight to each, reaching finally a compromise between what people want and what they ought to have. It would be hard to prove that the politicians and civil servants are particularly successful in making the right decision. What is manifest, however, is that theirs is an infinitely more difficult task than that which confronts the business man. We need not wonder if their decisions often prove wrong. We need not even register surprise at their inability to make any decision at all. To be Mayor of New York is a great honour, but we are mostly happy to leave that office to someone else. Whoever is Prime Minister of East Bengal is safe from any competition on our part. When a Secretary-General to the United Nations has next to be appointed the author of this book will not be offended at the deliberate omission of his name from the short list. Whether attainable or not, many political offices are not even attractive.

There are, then, at least three basic differences between business men and politicians and these are differences, moreover, which have existed from the time of the earliest to that of the most recent civilization. For most periods of history known to us the merchant, banker or industrialist has been clearly subordinate to the government, entitled to make representations, able to protest, but forced in the end to accept even the most unwelcome developments of policy. Where there has been serious friction it has been the result of the business organization becoming too big for its country of origin and base of activity; or else—from another point of view— it has resulted from the country remaining too small. Why should there be this disproportion? Or why, in other words, should business organizations tend to grow in size? There may be several causes but the first and often the most important is clearly the quest for security through vertical integration. The industrialist or merchant will normally attempt to gain control of his sources of supply and then again of his trade outlets. The more he feels responsible to investors and employees, the less can he risk being left without raw materials or markets. What if his suppliers sold to someone else? What if the wholesale merchants bought from someone else? He does not feel safe until his control extends from one end of the trade route to the other. But this may mean that he is a power in the land with bigger resources than the State of which he is a citizen. It is also possible and indeed likely that his trade route will extend beyond the frontier, giving him an interest in another State and perhaps in several others. He bursts out of his original homeland like a chicken from an egg. There are then two alternatives, one being that his business comes to be nationalized, the other being that he takes over the government. In the days of the Italian City States the latter alternative was pursued in fifteenth-century Florence. There the Medici owners of the leading merchant bank assumed control of the public administration and retained control until well into the Eighteenth Century.

Today the pattern is repeated but on a larger scale and with certain complications. City States still exist but the Nation State is the accepted political pattern in Europe, a political unit designed solely for purposes of war, a unit of thirty to sixty million inhabitants, small enough to be politically unified but large enough to be effectively aggressive. For efficient administration it is too big, unless perhaps in a federal form. For industrial purposes it is certainly too small and does not always fit the economic pattern. Within its rigid frontiers the industrial organizations grow to a size which threatens to burst the framework. In U.S.A. the industrial groups are larger still but admittedly have more room to breathe. We should remember, nevertheless, that the big corporations are bigger and more important than many of the States in the Union. The President of General Motors is a more powerful man than the Governor of New Hampshire or Maine. The difference is, however, that one holds an official office while the other is merely head of a business group or what people sometimes call an industrial empire. There is a familiar kind of American motion picture in which politicians are shown as corrupt and spineless puppets, manipulated by their unseen masters, the men with the money. To what extent that picture is true no tactful European would claim to know but the relationship described is at least plausible to the American public. They have sensed a fact which few of them could accurately describe; the fact that the political theory does not fit in with the financial and economic fact. Whereas the early senators and congressmen represented rural communities in which farmers and frontiersmen could elect men they knew to political office, the whole picture is now totally different. These rural communities have mostly vanished, their place being taken by industrial units concerned with steel, rubber, plastics and oil. Theory and reality have drifted far apart. If congressmen from Michigan do not represent General Motors, it is fair to ask what they do represent? The big industrial group is a main feature of the landscape in all non-socialist countries with an advanced technology. It is almost too big to be noticed. And it is something of which our political consitutions seem to be completely unaware.

To illustrate this last point and underline its significance we need to grasp the fact that politics were often more realistic in earlier periods of history. The idea of the English House of Lords was to assemble the men thought to be powerful, the men who were too important to overlook, the men it would be dangerous to exclude. Their lordships comprised the King's immediate male relatives (legitimate or otherwise), the archbishops, the bishops and some of the abbots, the biggest landowners, the best soldiers and the best lawyers. Was it dangerous to assemble these powerful men? Experience proved that it was a great deal more dangerous to ignore them. This is still true to some extent and the House of Lords still exists with something of its original character. In most other countries the 'second chamber' if there is one, has come to be elected; which would seem to make it redundant. In no country known to us does the political structure find room for the leading industrialist as such. He can be elected to be sure, but vote-seeking is not usually a pastime for which the leader of industry has either the time or the taste. Nor have business men always succeeded as politicians when given public office. We have therefore become re-signed to a situation in which a country's ablest men may not be consulted at all about anything. It is arguable that this is an unfortunate state of affairs. It is arguable, even, that we should ask whether a remedy exists which we could apply.

Some may object that business interests are well represented in many of the world's legislatures and that presidents of leading countries, like U.S.A., have often been thought to be representatives of capitalism. It is a question, however, whether the democratically elected industrialist is still a representative of industry. For re-election he must depend upon the votes of constituents whose interests may differ from his. In Britain, at least, we have had experience of men with an industrial background acting, and perhaps, rightly, against the interests of the firms upon which their private fortunes were based. Could not the same be said of a Roosevelt or a Kennedy? It is sometimes urged among business

In no country known to us does the political structure find room for the leading industrialist

men that their elder colleagues should enter politics when they retire, bringing into government a knowledge, much needed, of finance. There are even politicians, like Mr. Edward Heath, in Britain, who bring leading industrialists into public administration, hoping for dramatic improvements in efficiency. These devices sometimes succeed but as often fail. Few do well in politics or public administration who take office after the age of sixty and few countries, apart from Britain, have any method of rewarding the industrialist who comes thus to his country's aid. By the time, finally, that the industrialist succeeds as a politician he has usually lost touch with his old colleagues, friends and rivals.

As contrasted with the politician the business man thinks internationally, thinks in terms of the balance sheet and puts before himself a relatively simple goal. On entering national politics he has to discard these three characteristics and, having discarded them, has no distinctive contribution to make. He becomes a politician but is often, unlike his rivals, a bad politician, inexperienced and vulnerable. If the world's major industrialists are to make a contribution to the direction of human affairs, they must do it within their own terms of reference, within the framework of their own thinking. They must work on an international level. They must lay the greatest stress on economy in the narrower sense —the avoidance of wasted effort or time or material resources. They must concentrate on the vital issues, simple in themselves, which politicians avoid because of their lack of appeal to the electorate. Finally, they should seek to establish an authority at world level, a United Nations version of the British House of Lords.

There is already in existence, as we know, the United Nations Conference on Trade and Development (UNCTAD). The weakness in this and the weakness of every United Nations activity centres upon that fatal letter N. The League of Nations died because it was a league of nations not of peoples. Least of all was it a league of people who had anything in common. The United

Nations will die of the same disease—nationalism. What might prove to be of more obvious value would be a world organization of Big Business, an annual conference of the world's major industrial groups, a meeting to be held without a single politician in the room. We have also to realize, at this stage, that an industry nationalized is—from this point of view—an industry that has ceased to exist. It is always surprising that, when the argument comes up about nationalization—what effect will it have on prosperity, welfare and industrial relations?—no one ever seems to point out that an organization which might be of world significance is thus dragged down to the level of the town council. The act of nationalization is nationalistic—almost parochial—in character. What the world needs is more of an international outlook and more people who are prepared to look at problems from an international point of view. Shell and Esso lead the way and we do well to realize that in world affairs (as in other fields of enterprise) the best lubricant is probably Oil.

CHAPTER 4

Our Overheads are Overhigh

There was no doubt a period in history when managers, concerned about wage levels, were unlikely to worry too much about the cost of administration. The recent trend towards greater mechanization has had the effect of reducing the proportionate numbers of the 'blue-collar' as opposed to the 'white-collar' staff. Of the total numbers on the payroll the clerical staff now forms a high and expensive proportion. It is natural, therefore, that we ask ourselves whether something might be achieved by the application of work measurement to overhead costs. Could there be a new source of profit, derived not from increasing the volume of business nor from lowering the cost of production, but simply through a reduction of overheads? Without some special effort in this area it is obvious that the cost of paperwork will tend to rise. One cause of this tendency lies in the fact that the workload is variable. The volume of business is subject to seasonal fluctuations due to climate and weather, the problems of transportation and industrial dispute, the sessions of politics, education and law, and the anomalies of the Christian, Muslim and Hindu calendars. Spasms of activity are followed by periods of idleness, the latter made more frequent by the incidence of the bottleneck, delay over one thing leading to delay over everything else. Given such a known fluctuation, the permanent staff is nearly always established at the highest level, to cope with the peak load. Managers fear to lose business through inability to transact it. To be over-staffed, they feel, is to play safe.

It was never his ambition to eliminate the rats

Overstaffed in relation to the slack period, the typical organization is resigned to the fact that some people on some days will be
relatively idle. But are they allowed to remain idle? There are
supervisors who realise that habits of idleness are all too easily
acquired. Their remedy is to make work. In the navy this used to
mean scrubbing the decks and polishing the brasswork. In the army
it used to mean cleaning out the stables and putting a shine on the
harness. In commerce it means checking the inventory, stock-
taking and balancing the accounts to the last halfpenny. A real
expert can thus ensure that the slack period ends with everyone
exhausted. Lacking such expertise, however, people will be idle
and with results which the management may not have foreseen.
For while people are happy to be idle for half their time they become worried when there is less to do than that. If work is not
found for them by the management they begin at this point to
find it for themselves. All sorts of work can be duplicated and
counter-checked, listed and rearranged. All sorts of plans can be
drawn up to deal with improbable eventualities. All this fuss and
bother might seem harmless but the sad fact is that pseudo-work
has a demoralizing effect. It is more than a waste of money. It is the
cause, rather, of inefficiency when the next peak of activity is
reached. When the crisis comes the pseudo-active are not even
available. Even when re-deployed they tend to be useless, their
habit being to do everything by the slowest method. This is not a
practice they will abandon overnight. The result is that the busy
period is made the occasion for hiring additional staff. These too
will be idle later and so the cycle repeats with more and more
people doing less and less work.

The answer to the problem of the fluctuating workload is of
course simple and obvious. The wise manager hires temporary
staff during the peak period of activity, discarding them after the
crisis has passed. This is what the Post Office has always had to do
at Christmas. Its wider application depends upon the temporary
staff being provided by specialized firms such as those which

operate so successfully in U.S.A. and Britain, as also nowadays in the other industrialized parts of Europe. This skilled service rests upon the fact that peak periods of activity are not simultaneous in different industries. It is thus found that housewives are available for part-time temporary work in winter, university students in summer. With a little organization and forethought the needs of industry can be met. We should be wrong, however, to conclude that this is the whole answer to the problem. By employing temporary staff we may prevent the increase of clerical staff which might otherwise result from fluctuation in the workload. But overheads can become overhigh for other reasons. Three separate but inter-connected causes can be recognized, the first of which is clearly the growth in size of organizations, the result of amalgamation and mergers. The second is the technique of control as applied by head office. The third is the stress laid on cost control as applied to things, contrasting with a more casual approach to costs as applied to time. The total volume of paper to be processed is governed largely (though not entirely) by these three factors. And it is this total volume that we should seek to reduce.

The growth in size of the organization is at least connected with the fact that equipment of growing sophistication implies a rising scale of investment. When it comes to the manufacture of a modern jet engine there may be only two or three firms in the world which are capable of making it at all. That only the giants are able to tender is not the result of a plot against the smaller firms; it results merely from the fact that the complexity of the task involves the highest level of high finance. Aerospace technology affords no real scope to the village blacksmith and as little to the market town bank manager. For this and for other reasons we now have some very large industrial groups. Their size brings with it a new complexity of organization, the mere proliferation of which is best explained as the result of people making work for each other. On this subject the theory has been put forward that any office which can boast a thousand employees is likely to be administratively self-sufficient. This technical term is used to describe a headquarters which needs no units to administer, no other offices with which to correspond, no outside contacts of any sort. Such an office can live on the paper it produces, its executives spending their time in reading each other's memoranda. Its staff will tend to multiply, moreover, on principles totally unconnected with the amount of work, if any, that has to be done. So long as the status of an executive can be measured by the number of his subordinates, so long will the head office grow and ramify, adding eternally to the cost of overheads.

The mere size, however, of head office is of less consequence than the technique of control which it applies to the branches. This technique cannot be understood except in its historical context. In the headquarters established centuries ago the chief object was always to assert and maintain authority over the organization as a whole. The task involved was all but impossible because of the distances to be covered and the relatively slow means of communication available. All the head office tradition has been to battle against these physical limitations, seeking always to control. There was no danger a century ago of over-centralization because head office lacked the means. Correspondence took months to come, the information received being out-of-date and the resulting directives being inapplicable by the time they arrived. Then, quite abruptly, the situation altered. As from about 1870 the means of control, hitherto feeble, were dramatically improved. There came successively the telegraph, the steamship, and, soon afterwards, the telephone. There followed the radio, the tele-printer, the car, the aircraft and, finally, the computer. Given the tools with which to assert himself, the chief executive's instinct was to use them to the full. At last he could do what had always been impossible. He could now exact the fullest information and issue the most detailed directions, feeling at last that his subordinates had all been fairly brought to heel. And the effectiveness of his control could be measured in tons of paper comprising statistics, returns, reports and accounts; regulations, instructions, exhortations and advice. The attempt to centralize will end, inevitably, in over-centralization.

The first effect of over-centralization is to kill all initiative on the periphery of the organization. The second result, perhaps less obvious, is to kill all leisure at the centre. The paper arrives in a quantity directly related to the degree of centralization that is being imposed. The office staff must be large enough to cope with the flood (if only to file it) and regulations, accounts and returns have a known tendency to breed and multiply. Suppose that a return is required of towels used in the company's washrooms, the originator of this process will seldom remember to specify a return for last month. He merely asks for a return, forgetting that things are easier to start than stop. Twenty years later this return will still be coming in. Nobody will know how it began or what it is for. No one will have looked at it or drawn any conclusion from it. Or suppose that a high executive calls for returns of absenteeism throughout the group, here again something is started which no one remembers to stop. But this apparently purposeful inquiry reveals another factor in the situation. Any institution, group or office will soon acquire a life of its own, a personality and tradition, a will to survive and a will to grow. To send for the statistics of absenteeism is unwittingly to start a process. In a few weeks time the absenteeism statistics section will need more clerks as well as more filing cabinets, more finance and more space. It is also the rule that the statistics collected will become more elaborate as time goes on. The question will be asked whether absenteeism is more characteristic of male or female, old or young, married or single, protestant or catholic, freemasons or elks. Is it related to climate or latitude or height above sea level? Is it affected by the moon or the tide or the football results? The Absenteeism Statistics Section is now a DEPARTMENT with analysts, wall-charts and confidential files. The scope of its work expands and ramifies but nothing is done to reduce or abolish absenteeism. Why not? Because the abolition of the evil to be investigated would kill the department itself—which would be absurd.

In public administration there is the same sort of process but without the potential danger of the balance sheet. Confronted by the allegedly growing evil of (say) pornography, the government will hold an inquiry and when convinced that action is necessary, will possibly form an Anti-Pornographic Department. Its officials will admit to no special interest in the subject ('I don't even possess a pornograph,' says the Permanent Under-Secretary when interviewed) but they resolve to leave no stone unturned, never shrinking from the sight of what may lie beneath. But the significant fact about the Permanent Under-Secretary is, above all, his permanence. He sees a career ahead of him with a pension at the end. It used to be said of the ratcatcher (now the rodent control officer) that he would always release two rats before finally quitting the infested warehouse. It was never his ambition to eliminate the rats. His idea was rather to conduct a continuous campaign against them, knowing that a too decisive victory would leave him unemployed. In the same way the formation of a Department-for-the-abolition-of is equivalent to guaranteeing-the-survival-of. For no team can survive without an opposing team, the porn-breakers needing the porn-brokers just as the police need the criminals. Should there be any real danger, however, of the evil's disappearance, it can always be revived—and certainly will be revived—by a new definition of what we have agreed to deplore. Much ingenuity will be shown by men whose careers are at stake.

So much for the process of control as extended from head office, with all the paperwork which it entails. But the work load is also affected by a third factor—the traditional emphasis on things as opposed to time. The historic obsession of the head office is with equipment, machines, goods and tools. This mental attitude dates back to a period when wages were low and tools were relatively expensive. Things matter because they can be shown on the credit side of a balance sheet, subject to depreciation but still an asset.

People appear only on the debit side as a continual expenditure. So our great aim is to check the inventory and detect pilfering of things like carbon paper and envelopes. This obsession has played a great part in the history of British hospitals, these peculiar institutions which incongruously unite aspects of life in the convent and the army. From the convent derived the idea that matrons, sisters and nurses are idealistic ladies who need not be paid and whose time can be regarded, therefore, as worthless. From the army came a military obsession with the keeping of accounts and the checking of stores. The result has been that nobody until very recently tried to cost the nurses' time, which has too often been spent in counting the pillow cases and sheets. The discovery that the nurses' time spent in checking the inventory is worth more than the missing chamber-pot is something very recent in hospital practice.

So much for the more obvious factors in the situation which results in our overheads being over-high. It would be natural to ask at this point what remedy can be found. It may be doubtful whether the same policy could be applied to every case but an actual instance of a reduction in overheads might at least suggest that a cure is known. The story which follows concerns the organization of a retail chain which specializes mainly in clothing. Our narrative begins at the moment when the chairman of the board wandered into a small branch store in an unimportant provincial town. He did so rather late on a Saturday afternoon and he found it difficult at first to gain anyone's attention. The situation was that familiar one in which everyone is trying to organize the business but nobody has any time for the customer. The chairman finally interrupted the work by introducing himself. He then asked the obvious question: 'What are you all doing?' He was presently assured that the staff were busy with catalogue cards. 'What do you do with them?' asked the chairman, who was told with a touch of impatience, 'We fill them in.' 'Why?' he persisted. 'Well, that is all that you can do with a catalogue card. It is made to be filled in.'

'Show me,' he said, and a card was brought to him. Examining the thing with care he was still at a loss, unable to see what useful purpose it could serve. And this incident started a new train of thought. If this piece of paper was useless, how many other pieces of paper might be equally useless? How much rubbish was in circulation and at what total cost in time and effort? There began a process of investigation and the eventual result was to eliminate, annually, some twenty million pieces of paper.

This drastic reduction of overheads was based on three principles which any business man might do well to memorize. The first principle is this: trust the local manager. The head office executives should not try to keep him on a tight leash. If he is incompetent he should be fired. But if he is fit to be manager at all he is also fit to be trusted. Do not pester him with demands for information. Do not heap his desk with directives and reproofs. Should you make that mistake, the head office's desks will be ten times as cluttered, the managing director being pinned to his by mere weight of correspondence. Such a chief executive, the victim of his own routine, has no chance to discover what is going on. All he can do is to empty the IN tray before he leaves in the evening—thus reaching the point at which his day's work should have *begun*. Perhaps the most significant fact in the story about the retail chain is that the chairman of the board had found time to visit an actual store on a Saturday afternoon. If he devoted all his attention to matters of higher policy he would never have seen a catalogue card. His success on this occasion was due to the fact that he had left himself time to look around.

The second principle is this: trust the girls behind the counter. Until the period of which we are speaking this retail firm had a system of internal invoices. The salesgirl who had sold out some category of stock was expected to fill in a form, obtain the signature of the supervisor and the initials of the assistant manager, deliver one copy to the office and take the original to the stockroom—by which time the potential customer would have gone home to tea. It was now decided to simplify the process. The sales-girl who had run short of goods was in future to go to the stock-room, fetch some more, put them on the counter and sell them. The apparent objection to this procedure was that the salesgirl might pilfer the stock. The objection was properly overruled on two grounds. It was pointed out, first of all, that the girls employed by the firm are perfectly honest. It was then pointed out that the new procedure would *still* be cheaper even if the girls were dis-honest. The actual cost of the paperwork exceeded any possible loss by petty theft.

The third principle is this: trust the customer. Until this time the aggrieved housewife—whose garment was of the wrong size or colour—was invited to fill in a complaint form, which had then to be presented at the store from which the goods had been pur-chased. The form was an impressive document in which some thirty-seven questions were numbered, beginning with 'Who was your grandfather and why?' When completed, the form would be studied, countersigned, stamped and checked, the decision being finally reached that the goods should be changed or the money refunded. It was now decided to abolish the complaint form. In future the aggrieved customer could take the goods back to *any* store in the chain—not of necessity the store at which they had been bought—and put them on the counter. They would then be changed or the money handed back without question or argument. This again was not a matter of benevolence. It resulted rather from having costed the paperwork. The time spent on processing the complaint form cost more than the value of the average garment. To trust the customer—and especially to refrain from arguing with the customer—would be at once kinder and cheaper; and that has been the policy ever since.

CHAPTER 5

Advertise or Perish

At school or college it was the fate of most of us to study, in passing, the Principles of Economics. Some reference to this fact has already been made (see p. 3)—reference, moreover, to a theory which seems to be at least plausible. Another principle, found nearer the beginning of the textbook, reads somewhat as follows: 'The Demand creates the Supply.' We are told, in effect, to picture the plight of primitive man when confronted by an angry elephant or dinosaur. 'What I want,' he said to himself, 'is a weapon with which I may shoot this creature from a safe distance.' His widow would afterwards express the same thought in the past tense. 'What he needed was the right weapon. I must see to it that my next husband is better equipped.' She then sent for a catalogue and found, on page 17, a picture of a bow and arrow. Or else it was her new husband who sat down in the cave and worked the whole thing out from first principles, coming up finally with the sketch of a blow-pipe or catapult. In later life we have come mostly to realize that what economists say is almost invariably wrong. Never, moreover, were they more mistaken than in this rubbish about the demand creating the supply. In point of fact, all historical example goes to prove the exact opposite; that it is nearly always the supply (if not the supplier) that creates the demand. This must be obvious almost as soon as stated, for very few people can imagine what they have not seen. In history the usual process is for someone to have a surplus or by-product, a load of something

Very few people can imagine what they have not seen

left on his hands, a pile of straw, a heap of goatskins or wool. We know this as a fact but we could as easily have guessed it. For the mental effort of deciding what to do with something you possess is relatively easy, whereas to decide what you want—never having seen it or anything like it—is for most people impossible. We are justified, therefore, in reversing the first principle we were taught. It is obvious, surely, that the Supply creates the Demand.

Historically, then, it is the seller who comes first. The traveller or merchant with camel, donkey or packhorse, has something to sell. He may incidentally buy things; but his first motive was to unload something he did not want or something of which he already had more than enough. We can also assume that his first task was always to explain the usefulness of what he had to offer. There could be no demand, initially, for goods which no one had ever seen before. It was the seller's task to explain to the potential purchaser that he had the opportunity of a lifetime but that similar opportunities would undoubtedly be offered from year to year. For if the supply were not to continue in some form, the simple folk he met would probably decide to kill him and take his goods without payment. So he would be anxious, at the outset, to emphasize the continuity of the supply. From the early dawn of history, therefore, there has been advertisement, and the essential points of the advertisement have always been the same. The vendor is able to offer goods which are extremely useful or anyway desirable. They are better and cheaper than the goods offered by anyone else. They can be replaced, as necessary, from the same source of supply. Bought in quantity, the goods can be had more cheaply than if bought singly and it may not always be essential to make immediate payment for them in full. The fact that the vendor will be here again next year is proof that he believes in the quality of what he has to offer. He is evidently confident that there will be no ambush laid by disappointed customers. He is certain, rather, that people will be delighted to see him again and the more so if they can rely on the discount he gives only to his particular friends. He emphasizes, finally, that should he be unable to come in person, everyone can recognize his trade mark as the guarantee of quality, value and service. The sequence of the advertisement has always been the same but the first point is the most important. For the man who seeks to sell, say, pepper to people who have never heard of it, the first problem is how to explain that pepper is essential to the good life; a point that is doubtful and may not even be true. In that particular instance the vendor's success was complete; and yet it might be difficult to show what disaster would follow were pepper to become suddenly unobtainable. We must conclude that the original advertising campaign for pepper must have been very effective indeed.

Since advertisement has this long and impressive history, stretching back to the earliest periods of which anything is known, it may seem odd that the advertising art is often regarded as new. It is new to this extent that people of today are more credulous, perhaps, than their ancestors. In most other respects the advertisement is what it always has been, technologically developed only in the means by which the message is made known to the public. This development began almost exactly a century ago, when the first advertising agencies were founded. As from that period specialists have given their whole attention and spent their whole lives in the planning of advertisements, designing the means by which attention can best be gained and discussing the form in which the advertiser's message can best be conveyed. A century ago the advertising profession had its origin, and immediately afterwards came the invention of the cheap paper upon which the agencies would henceforth be able to rely. From about 1870 dates the paper flood by which the world is still submerged, advertisements rivalling in quantity even the circulars sent out by the ministries. It became essential at the same time to send people to school, without which precaution written advertisements would have been wasted on the illiterate. Nowadays, however, even illiteracy (which is growing) is no protection, for the advertisement is as often spoken as printed. Whether we like it or not, advertisement has become an inescapable part of the world in which we live. Industrialized society would be impossible without it.

What is the first principle of advertising? If any one were to be given pride of place, it might be the rule that: 'No amount of advertisement will sell what is not saleable.' It is true that better advertising will persuade the public to choose product 'A' rather than 'B', assuming that both will serve the purpose for which they are sold. That does not mean, however, that the public can for long be tricked into buying what is dearer and worse. If there is an exception to this rule it is in the field of enterprise where the article sold is little more than a dream; the perfume which will make a plain girl beautiful, the medicine which will restore the vitality of youth, the holiday resort at which romance is guaranteed. Remember, however, that a dream is still saleable and that the advertising agency has done no more than persuade the customer to prefer one dream to another. The basic principle remains that the thing sold must be saleable and perhaps we should add that the advertising experts must themselves believe in it. Let us reject from the outset the idea that advertising men are without scruple. They are rather in the position of contending advocates in a Court of Law, most of them men whose integrity is beyond question. Before that court the advertising men say all that they can for their respective clients, using every persuasion that they know. When they have finished let us remember that the public is the judge and one against whose verdict there is no appeal.

It is the complaint among socialists that advertisements trick people into buying what they do not need and cannot afford. While there may be some truth in this the fact remains that modern industry could not exist without the modern advertisement. It is also a generally accepted fact that a business must either expand or decay. There is no such thing as a static enterprise for the firm which wants only its accustomed share of the market will soon be elbowed out by firms which want an increasing share.

Some, not all, of this elbowing-out process is done through the medium of advertising. So much is obvious, but what people often forget is the extent to which sales may be affected by quite different products. The brewer of beer is apt to regard some other brewer as his chief rival in the market. His real rival is the manufacturer of ice-cream. Book publishers see themselves as in competition with each other. They are in fact competing with the builders of sailing boats and the makers of tennis rackets, card games and skis; with all, in fact, who purvey entertainment in any other form. If the brewers advertise and the publishers do not, the additional money spent on beer will not be available for books. So the influence of advertising is more pervasive than people suppose. Except in the heaviest industries the manufacturers, the merchants and the retailers must use all the available means of publicity. The business man must, in fact, use every advertising tool that lies to hand—television, radio, newspaper, magazine and poster. What he neglects will be used by his rivals. In a word, he must advertise or perish.

Advertisement most commonly takes the form of a direct approach to the public. Using some chosen medium, the vendor proclaims that Washwell Soap is the best or anyway the cheapest. He can use argument or he can just reiterate the name until a hypnotized public can think of no other brand. He can use either blatant or hidden persuasion. He can play on the basic instincts of snobbery or sex. He can appeal to gamblers with lucky serial numbers and free trips to the Bahamas. He can use scientific means to achieve a well-defined purpose. He can also, however, go wildly astray. One quite common mistake, for instance, is to sell what you do not stock. This happens with astonishing frequency; the premature advertisement of things which have not arrived. This is the worst kind of backfire, leaving your customer to decide whether you are more fool or knave. Have you done it merely to annoy them? Or are you just feeble-minded, unfit to do business at all? All your twitterings about the mistake made by the advertising firm are waste of breath. The basic fact remains that you were trying to sell what you did not possess. It is an unpardonable sin against all the ethics of the market place.

A rather similar crime is to advertise something which may actually exist but which cannot be found. This is especially common in cities which have grown rapidly from an original village. Fifty years ago, Messrs Dopey and Snoring were the only hardware merchants in Hogwash. A letter addressed to Dopey and Snoring, Inc., Hogwash City, Omega, U.S.A., would have been delivered then without a second's hesitation. It remains the illusion, therefore, of Snoring's son-in-law (the present manager) that everyone in the State must know that his business premises are at 32nd Street on Sycamore. There are now, however, 350,000 inhabitants of Hogwash and at least nine other hardware merchants, three of them in Sycamore Avenue. Advertising their Annual Sale the D. & S. executives lay stress on the unrepeatable bargains which they, and they alone, can offer. Each double-page two-colour spread ends with the stirring slogan, 'We have it—yes! At D & S!' All that they forget to add is their postal address and telephone number. If challenged, they would protest that their store has been on the same corner since 1885, and that everyone knows where it is. But this is no longer true. While the *store* has been there the present *inhabitants* have mostly been somewhere else. Many came to the city a year ago and will leave in another twelve months. Many live out in Overspill and visit the down-town area about once a year, to see the Christmas display. True, they could look up the address in the telephone book. But will they bother? Besides, mother may see the advertisement while driving with father to the airfield. 'Dopey and Snoring', she asks, 'Where could they be?' Her husband has never heard of the store and her eye is immediately caught by another advertisement, this time for Budget Week at the Overspill Supermarket. That is where she calls on the way home for she knows where it is. D & S have lost another potential customer. A re-worded slogan, 'We have it—yes—*at this address*! might have brought her into the store.

Another crime against the advertising art is to choose a brand name which no one can pronounce. There was once a brushless shaving cream called RAZVITE, a word well chosen to suggest a minimal time in the bathroom. Impressed by the give-away sample, a customer would ask the drugstore for a tube of RAZ-VITE (to rhyme with stays-white). He would be met with a look of blank incomprehension. After some minutes of exasperation on either side the superior young lady behind the counter would suddenly guess his meaning. 'Ah!! You mean RAZVITE' (to rhyme with car's seat)! After some further period spent in sniggering at his ignorance and telling the other girls about it, she would complete the deal. Amidst suppressed but audible laughter the crestfallen customer would creep out of the store. Three weeks later, his lesson learnt, he would ask for RAZVITE (to rhyme with car's seat) at another store. The chemist, a man this time, would stare at him with a puzzled expression. Eventually he would exclaim, 'Oh!—you mean RAZVITE!' (to rhyme with stays-white) and go off chuckling to fetch it from the back of the store. Three weeks later again, the same customer would be asking for *Robinson's* Shaving Cream. It might be more expensive and it might be worse but people would at least know what he was talking about. To choose a brand name which cannot be mispronounced would seem to be an obvious precaution. It is surprising, however, that this most elementary of rules should be broken again and again.

Distinct from the direct appeal to the public is the news item which comes from a seemingly unbiased source. The Cosmic Cosmetic Corporation invites Olga Orloff (the film star) to open the new extension to their Connecticut factory. The account of her visit is carried by the editorial rather than the advertising pages of the press. She looks radiant in all the pictures—with the factory in the background. She is seen receiving a bouquet of flowers—with the general manager beside her. She is photographed as she replies to the speech of welcome—with the Cosmic Cosmetic banner just over her head. She is interviewed at her hotel—and admits that Cosmic is the only brand whe would *dream* of using. Appearing on television, she attributes her success to Cosmic; but for which she would still be an Off-Broadway understudy. There may be (who knows?) a few who doubt her sincerity; but the general assumption is that her enthusiasm is unprompted and unrewarded. She and Cosmic are just good friends. Having discovered the world's best lipstick, she naturally wants to tell the world about it. This sort of publicity is in some way the best, for the message seems to come from someone who is not financially interested in the sale.

There are times when the advertisement with the widest influence is genuinely unintentional. The President of Ruritania quite innocently may remark at his airfield press conference that he had a most comfortable flight with Paneurasian Airways. He may even say it with the aircraft behind him and pretty hostess handing him his hat. Such incidents do actually occur, and who would grudge the airline such extra profit as may result? But airline publicity is closely connected with holiday advertising in general, the multi-million message about where to go and how to travel. It is easy to visit the travel agency and come away with an armful of brochures about fantastically attractive and economical holidays to be enjoyed in Majorca and Malta, in Cyprus and Spain. These are organized by a number of different firms set up for the purpose, one being called (shall we say?) Mayfair Travel and another (shall we agree?) Happiday Holidays Ltd. The Mayfair brochure is smartly produced with a good type face on good paper, with excellent photography and well-drawn sketch maps of the Costa Lotta. The Happiday brochure is a poorly produced affair in which all the hotels look exactly the same, each represented by an identical shot of what seems to be the same swimming pool. The girl on the cover is slightly overweight with a provincial accent which the camera has somehow managed to catch. The beaches shown in garish colour are all revoltingly overcrowded and several pages of the brochure are stuck together with an evil-smelling glue. The whole effect is subtly unattractive and we toss the thing on one side. Mayfair, now, has a certain air of distinction. Take, for example, the description it provides of the Hotel Classica at Puerta de la Cruz. There is a telling description of its amenities, a cleverly angled shot of its courtyard and a picture of a cocktail party on the moonlit terrace with pretty frocks and tropical evening dress. We decide that this offers what we want.

Having made that tentative decision, we think again. Why should we be so influenced by the style in which the brochure is published? Is there not a risk that Mayfair, having overspent at the printers, may have economized on something else? As against that it might be argued that people unable to produce an attractive brochure are as incapable, most probably, of producing anything else. They will have misprinted the time of departure, booked us at a hotel which does not exist and sent the limousine to meet a flight on last year's schedule. Apart from that, people who choose the wrong pictures will almost certainly pick the wrong hotel at the wrong resort. To illustrate this point, we pick up the discarded brochure and point scornfully to this page and that. What a repulsive-looking monstrosity of a place shown on page fifteen! Who in his senses would book a holiday in such vulgar surroundings? Still in a critical mood, we tear open the pages which were stuck together. . . . We don't suppose for a moment that we missed anything worth considering but just in case. . . . There! You see? More of those crowded beaches and concrete barracks! Look at this ghastly . . . ghastly . . . Good God! It is the Hotel Classica at Puerta de la Cruz! What is there left to say? But nevertheless we make the booking through Mayfair, still half-convinced that this agency will have better rooms to offer. This proves once more that it pays to advertise and proves even more that it pays to advertise *well*.

CHAPTER 6

The Consultants

The adviser on Organization and Method is sometimes called an efficiency expert and sometimes an industrial engineer but the more descriptive term—that of management consultant—seems to be gaining ground. Similar progress is being made by the profession itself, which is slowly gaining acceptance among business men whose first reaction was often sceptical and is sometimes sceptical even now. The doubts felt by many are well expressed by Robert Townsend in these words:

MANAGEMENT CONSULTANTS

The effective ones are the one-man shows. The institutional ones are disastrous. They waste time, cost money, demoralize and distract your best people, and don't solve problems. They are people who borrow your watch to tell you what time it is and then walk off with it.[1]

Robert Townsend's advice is not to be ignored; but neither should it be followed without question. The trouble is that he happens to be a very remarkable man. When he says that we should fire the whole P.R. Department—and indeed abolish it—he is describing what he did and was wise to do. The policies he recommends would not of necessity succeed as well with a chief executive

[1] *Up the Organization*, Robert Townsend, New York 1970 (p. 104).

who is not Robert Townsend. A less colourful character might be well advised to pursue a less drastic policy. A more modest man might do well to seek advice from a consultant. And yet even he might hesitate. Why, he could ask, should any outside person be in a position to tell the directors of a company how their business should be organized? If they don't know, who does? And if they don't know, for what are they being paid? The consultant, for that matter, has no qualification which makes it reasonably certain that his advice is worth having. He probably began as an accountant, lawyer, or engineer. After some experience he becomes a consultant, a self-appointed expert in management. How do we know that he is as clever as he thinks he is? Granted, moreover, that he *is* clever, why is he not a leader of industry? As they say in America, 'If you're so smart, why aren't you rich?'

This last question is the easiest to answer, for while there are examples of ex-consultants who have succeeded in business, the born consultant would never attempt it. He knows that his mind is on a different wavelength. Like a psychologist, his concern is with other people's affairs. Like an actor, he has to throw himself into a part. 'What should I do' (he asks himself) 'if I were the manager of this factory?' 'What would be my gesture at this moment' (asks the actor) 'if I were Hamlet, Prince of Denmark?' Between the actor and the prince there is a sharp distinction for the prince has to be himself and the actor has to be someone else. It is our realization of this fact that makes us apprehensive when a well-known actor is interviewed on television and sometimes asked his opinion on some issue of the day. For we all know instinctively (as the interviewer does not) that a good actor has no opinion on any subject outside the theatre. What opinions *can* a man have who has to play the parts successively of king and anarchist, of cardinal and colonel? Let him once identify himself with a cause, however noble, and he must fail in portraying a character whose views are meant to be totally opposed. Off stage the best players are often faceless, nondescript and tongue-tied. In the same way the good consultant is often a failure in running his own consulting business, his daily attention being given to every business but that. It was said of a certain professor of architecture that he was one of the most inspiring teachers in the world but that any building he actually designed—even were it no more than a public lavatory—would certainly have collapsed before it could even be used. Like the signpost by the roadside, the born consultant points the way but does not follow it.

A consultant, then, may do everything but mind his own business. We can still fairly ask how he can claim to understand ours. In what sense is he an expert? His answer must be that his experience mostly relates to the time of crisis. The ordinary company director may work steadily for years without having to decide any big question of policy. He may have to face a major decision only once or twice during the whole of his career. Should his company expand its business or move into another field of enterprise? Should he sell out to a larger organization? Should he diversify the product or seek new markets for the goods that are currently being produced? These moments of dramatic decision, coming (say) three times in the less eventful business career, come each week for the consultant. Knowing little at the outset, he comes to gain experience in a concentrated form. The analogy to consider is that of a merchant seaman and the skipper, by contrast, of a salvage tug. On an average one might guess that an elderly merchant seaman might have been present on one or two occasions when a ship has gone aground. He has, therefore, only a rough idea of what to do in such an emergency. But the skipper of a salvage tug rarely has to do with a ship which is NOT aground. He is present at every disaster and goes to every shipwreck. For him there is a new catastrophe every month and he may have little experience of anything else. In the same way the management consultant is familiar with the crises which occur in industry. To change the metaphor, he has the expert knowledge of the surgeon in a casualty ward. Moments of crisis are to him a matter of routine. Like the surgeon, he comes to know the symptoms of concussion, fracture and shock.

It is by some such analogies as these that one can explain the value of a consultant's experience. Five years' work as a consultant is the equivalent of fifty years in ordinary business because the whole of that period has been devoted to the most difficult problems. At the outset the consultant may know little more than his client but he works, as a junior, alongside a man whose knowledge is considerable. As time goes on, moreover, he learns from the clients themselves, and especially from their mistakes. In business the consultant is like the bee which goes from plant to plant, pollinating each for the benefit of all. He comes to know the quality of the plant at a glance. How? Well, this is a trade secret and readers are asked to keep it to themselves, but the consultant always looks, first of all, at the girl who occupies the reception desk. If the management cannot find an attractive girl for the outer office it seems most unlikely that they will have found anything else. Remember, however, that she must be attractive in the right way. She can charm, and she should, but she must not distract. His second glance should take in the number of directors on the board. To have more than eleven is a bad symptom but to have more than nineteen is a sign of approaching collapse. His third glance is at the age of the directors. Ours is an era, we are told, when the accent is on youth. It has also been the age of Macmillan and Nehru, of Adenauer and Chairman Mao, of Chiang Kai-shek and Charles de Gaulle. These heirs of the Jet-Age, these godlike wielders of the nuclear thunderbolt were all born between 1876 and 1894. Whether they are or were the ideal leaders—or whether they should have gone out with the horse-drawn vehicle—must be a matter of opinion. The effect they have had on their potential successors is a matter of fact.

The management consultant must be faced with a variety of problems from week to week and no two of them can be solved in exactly the same way. There is, nevertheless one principle upon which the competent consultant will normally insist, and it applies to almost any situation. The principle can be expressed in these words: 'The first concern of the good workman is to take care of his tools.' Faced with some frightful problem of our age—the overpopulation of the world, the colour question, the conflict between the major powers, the state of the economy, the prevalence of industrial dispute, the balance of trade—the first instinct of the politician or the citizen is to ask urgently, 'Should we do this or that?' The first instinct of the consultant is to ask, 'Are we so organized as to solve that problem or any other?' The expert's first concern is with method, with structure, with the deployment of our resources. The good general's first concern is with his own staff. His next care is to organize, equip and train his army. When all that has been done, with supplies at hand and ammunition ready, he decides at last on a plan of campaign. On the battlefield the young recruit may wonder whether the enemy will attack from the right or the left. The old soldier does not pretend to know. What he *does* know is that the rifles need to be zeroed, cleaned, oiled, inspected and loaded. Should our politicians call in a business consultant, asking him, 'What ought we to do?'; he would surely reply, 'Do nothing until you have put your own house in order'. Should they ask, 'Which way shall we go?' he might well observe that their aged and creaking organization is unfit to go in any direction. Unnoticed amidst the argument between those who want to go left and those who want to go still further left, the old car has collapsed by the roadside. It is for the consultant to point out, as he must, that it will never move again.

Another symptom of internal decay, and one the consultant learns to recognize, is the paper flood. Mention has already been made of this ailment, considered as an aspect of over-centralization (see p. 31). But even when the disease is endemic the good manager can learn to survive it. The consultant comes in fact to recognize the quality of management as applied to this particular problem. To illustrate this point the reader is asked to compare the daily routine of two high executives, one named (without much originality) B, and the other named (as unimaginatively) A. Each is the manager of an industrial group and neither is more than middle-aged. Their duties are broadly similar but their business methods are sharply contrasted. An experienced consultant would know at once to what category each of them belongs.

Manager B arrives at his office to find his in-tray piled high with files, documents, letters and memoranda. Before he can deal with more than three of these, the telephone rings and he has scarcely put down the receiver when his first caller arrives. Amidst continual interruption, he battles with the tide of paper, no sooner dealing with six items than the mail arrives with ten more. He struggles on, barely pausing for lunch, and by the late afternoon he has the situation under control. The pile in the in-tray has begun to shrink. It dwindles and vanishes and the last letters are signed. Late in the evening, long after everyone else has gone, Manager B rises stiffly from his chair with a sense of having won the battle. Every caller has been seen, every telephone call answered, and every incoming letter has elicited a reply. B feels that he has done well. Few others, he ventures to guess, could have done as much. Wearily he sets off for his home in Long Island or Hampstead.

But *has* he done well? The fact is that B has achieved nothing. He has allowed the paper flood to rob him of the initiative. His has been a purely defensive battle without time to learn or think or plan. And what if he should fall sick? Were we Dutch or resident in Holland, we should know all the stories which attach to a country below sea level. We should know about the efforts made to reclaim the land in the first place. We would be familiar with tales of disaster which centre upon the crisis when the sea breaks through, upon the heroism of the boy who sits on the leak, upon the Ministry's promise to give the problem a high priority and upon the statesman's grave decision in ordering the dykes to be opened in the face of a threatened invasion. Our picture is of a countryside below sea level with only a frail barrier between it and

He has allowed the paper flood to rob him of the initiative

the threatening waves. So it is with B's correspondence. Let him fall ill and the dykes will burst. Paper will pour into the office in a foaming torrent. It will overflow from his in-tray, cascade off his desk and swirl round his chair, the water level rising quickly from the floor towards the ceiling. After an absence of ten days, B cannot return at all. The office is full, the door won't close, the corridor is knee-deep and the paper is trickling down the staircase. There is nothing for him to do except commit suicide.

Contrast that with the day's work of Manager A. Beginning rather earlier in the day, he has answered fifty letters by 9.30, often scribbling 'yes' or 'no' on the letter he has received. Then he stops dead and makes six or eight telephone calls. At 9.50 he holds a staff conference, which lasts exactly ten minutes. At 10.0 he begins a tour of the factory, his real day's work begun. He sees everything and has a word with everyone, notes when a machine is too hot or where electricity is being wasted, observes the gutter that is blocked, asks the foreman whether his wife has come out of hospital, discovers the name of the new apprentice and ponders over a plan for changing the system by which the raw material is delivered. If there is discontent among the workers, Manager A sees it coming. If there is bad feeling between two departmental chiefs, A knows all about it. If the coffee in the works canteen is undrinkable, A will be the first to realize the fact. And should the factory catch fire, A would be the first on the spot with the hand appliance. For A, the correspondence which has B pinned to his desk is not the day's work but a mere interruption. His real work lies, he thinks, with people and things, not with paper; unless, of course, it should be paper that he is manufacturing. In the opinion of some people, Manager A is a very competent man indeed. He is of a type well known in industry. But we have to admit that Manager B is also not unknown, even here and even now. He exemplifies, surely, a type of failure which is becoming too common—the man who has retreated behind his desk, the man for whom his work has proved too much.

Administration becomes too often a matter of paper pushing, signing and initialling. Whether we are in government service or private interprise, we have the paper manufacturers to thank for it; or, anyway, some of them. But there is a difference between public and business administration. For behind the paper are people and things, some rare and expensive, some common and cheap; and it is in terms of these that we in business must succeed or fail. In the civil service a file is an end in itself. In business the end is a consolidated balance sheet with underlined grand total in black or in red. The meaning of the balance sheet may not always be obvious, but the meaning is there. If we have succeeded the final figure is the measure of our success. If we have failed our failure is there for all to see.

CHAPTER 7

Peter's Predicament

Peter's Principle has been given to the world with powerful publicity and many students of politics have been predictably impressed. His doctrine is, briefly, as follows: In a Hierarchy Every Employee Tends to Rise to his Level of Incompetence. Ours is a world, he points out, of incompetence rampant. So long as anyone works efficiently he is regarded as suitable for promotion. Successive promotions bring him to a level in the organization at which he proves incompetent, the work being beyond his ability. He is not, therefore, promoted again but is left where he is, unable as ever to cope with his duties. By this process (we are told) the majority of posts come to be filled by incompetent people who remain in office until they retire. At their level of incompetence employees are said to have reached Peter's Plateau and are given a Promotion Quotient (P.Q.) of ZERO. This basic trend is confused, the author admits, by apparent exceptions and variations. He thus happily describes such phenomena as the Lateral Arabesque, the manoeuvre by which the incompetent employee is given a longer title and moved to a more remote office. He points out that the symptoms of the Final Placement Syndrome include the obsession with side-issues (Structurophilia and the Edifice Complex, for example) and hierarchical regression. He embellishes his argument with aphorisms such as that 'If you don't know where you are going, you will probably end up somewhere else'. He claims that even computers are subject to the Peter Principle. His final advice is that we should all refuse promotion when at our level of competence, or else (and more subtly) ensure that no promotion is offered us. He thus triumphantly justifies 'The Power of Negative Thinking'.

There is much to admire in this chain of reasoning and it cannot be denied that the author has made some significant discoveries. His central doctrine is explained with lucidity and eloquence and his disciples are said to be numerous. There can be no doubt that he is an admirable and idealistic teacher, the author of a book that is deservedly successful. The trouble is that some people take the book too seriously, agreeing with a theory that was probably put forward as a joke. There is nothing to be said against the joke but there is one possible objection to his theory; the objection that it happens to be wrong. It does not accord with our actual experience, nor does it stand up to critical scrutiny. We have indeed to ask ourselves, at the outset, how the author came (if he did come) to believe in it? When we learn that he is or was Co-ordinator of Programs for Emotionally Disturbed Children at the University of Southern California we incline at first to suspect that the Peter Principle may well be one of the Programs he has managed to co-ordinate. That there are Emotionally Disturbed Children at his University need not surprise us and it could well be that one Program, among many, might also have its appeal to Emotionally Disturbed Adults. It would seem certain, however, that any such conclusion would be ill-considered and superficial.

The clue to Dr. Peter's thinking lies not in his former or current co-ordinating role (which represents no more than a Lateral Arabesque) but in his past career and his present assumptions. He is a schoolmaster and school psychologist (Ed.D) who has become an Associate Professor of Education in Southern California. The examples of incompetence given in his book begin with Excelsior City School System and revert to it at regular intervals with stories about school principals, teachers and educational administrators. Footnotes refer, moreover, to the author's other book on *Prescrip-*

tive Teaching (whatever that may be). Altogether, we are left in no doubt that the author's life has been mainly spent in the classroom and the educational hierarchy. He admittedly quotes some examples of incompetence from the worlds of public and business administration but without much hint of inner knowledge or previous research. Outside the Excelsior School System he moves, one feels, without confidence; a clergyman on his first visit to the casino. One may suspect, finally, that Excelsior City is in California, the State in which the expansion of the educational racket could almost be called an explosion. When he observes that 'Escalation of educational effort speeds the process of degradation', he carries instant conviction, but with special reference to California where the system of watering down the cream of scholarship first reached its logical conclusion. Behind the author and his theory there looms a significant and peculiar landscape.

The male schoolteacher in U.S.A. is a person left behind among the women and children after the men of the tribe have gone to work or war. He is taken from the least intelligent of those who undergo higher education, being only marginally superior to those who graduate in social studies. Once committed to his semi-adult occupation he learns 'How to take a Class in —' the last and vital word being left out. We all know that successful teaching beyond the infant class involves (a) wide and detailed knowledge of a difficult subject, (b) an enthusiasm for the subject which communicates itself to the class, and (c) a few simple tricks of the trade, learnt by anyone from a single volume and from about three weeks of experience. The art of the Educationalizer is to expand (c) into a mass of pretentious nonsense, fogged by technical terms and psychological twaddle. To do research in Educationalization is to forget about (a) and (b) and make the mastery of (c) seem practically impossible. Those who can, do (it has been said), and those who cannot will teach teachers how to teach other teachers the art of teaching. This is the brotherhood of the Ed.D. and it forms a sort of campus within the campus; an enclave, as it were, of people committed to the study of nothing. It is in these surroundings that Dr. Peter bewails the fact that most people are incompetent. He has lived most of his life, one suspects, in a world where that is literally true.

Others of us have had a different sort of experience. We have lived, some of us, among airmen, bankers, engineers, seamen, composers, soldiers and journalists; among many people, indeed, of an almost appalling competence. More than that, we have come to assume that most people we know are fully equal to the work they have undertaken. The pilot of the jet plane in which we travel is trusted implicitly by passengers who have not even seen him. The surgeon who removes our appendix is assumed to be skilful and sober and we have almost as much confidence in the mechanic who services our car. There are rare instances of navigators who steer their ship into fatal collision but the average ship's captain does nothing of the sort. There are engineers whose bridge falls into the river and this even happened once to a hydro-electric plant on the American side of Niagara Falls. We cross our bridges, nevertheless, with an unquestioning faith in their stability and a reliance which our experience would seem to justify. We may not have quite the same confidence in architects, plumbers and tax-collectors. We may have actual doubts about politicians, pop-singers and painters. The fact remains, however, that we assume the competence of most people with whom we have dealings and our trust is only occasionally misplaced.

So much for the practice, but what of the theory? Where does Dr. Peter's argument fall down? Its breakdown is over the word 'competent' on which the whole theory is made to hinge. As an educationalizer, Dr. Peter has been brought up to believe in the Intelligence Quotient or I.Q. In the Excelsior City School System the child's I.Q. is known and the teacher does not expect more from a pupil than his potential, as thus measured, would seem to foreshadow. The wise child will presumably fix himself a low I.Q. so as to gain the more credit from any subsequent success.

We have lived, some of us, among airmen, bankers, engineers, seamen, composers, soldiers and journalists

Cheating apart, the I.Q. is almost entirely controlled by heredity and is incapable, therefore, of improvement. The author of the Peter Principle uses the word 'competence' in the same way, assigning to each human being a 'ceiling' in terms of ability, a level above which he will prove incompetent. All (or nearly all) surpass their proper level, thus producing a hierarchy of this pattern:

Directors, competent only as Managers

Managers, good enough to be Assistant Managers,

Assistant Managers, fit only to be Foremen

Foremen, who would do as Charge Hands,

Charge Hands, competent merely as Workmen,

Workmen, unfit to be employed at all, and

Apprentices, unfit to live.

The fallacy in this chart is that no ordinary institution employs just four men on each level, the directors as numerous as the foremen, the workmen no more frequent than the charge hands. There has to be a president or managing director at the top and there have to be more people lower down. We come back in the end to the pyramid. There are exceptions to this pattern, as Dr. Peter seeks to emphasize, but some of them are more apparent than real. The commoner forms of organization must still have an apex and a base. The oblong shape inevitably becomes:

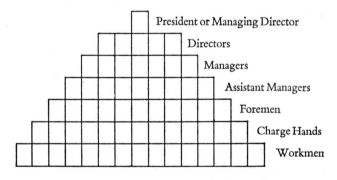

President or Managing Director

Directors

Managers

Assistant Managers

Foremen

Charge Hands

Workmen

This is a simplified organizational chart and the pyramid would soon assume a flatter, perhaps less regular, form. Even, however, were the numbers as shown and all eligible for promotion within the factory, there would only be the one President and a minimum of fifteen workmen. If we assume with Dr. Peter that the president is incompetent—being fit only for a directorship—we have to deduce either (a) that there was *nobody* fit for the top post, or, (b) that those who would have been suitable are lower in the organization and are therefore *below* their level of competence. When we realize, however, that of the sixty people below the rank of president, only two or three can succeed to that office as it falls vacant, we are forced to conclude that fifty-seven or fifty-eight are doomed to disappointment in the nature of things. Even were ten of them potential presidents, the majority of these would have to content themselves with office at a lower level. The narrowing of the pyramid holds people down irrespective of their competence. So far from being made directors when only fit to be managers, many will have to remain at the managerial level because there is no vacancy for them on the board. Given an oblong, the Peter Principle might at least be plausible. Given a pyramid, it is plainly incorrect.

Whatever the pattern of the organization, Peter's Principle assumes that each person's level of competence is as permanent as his height and blood group. But competence is not comparable to I.Q. While some failures and mishaps are due to an employee's basic lack of brain, the majority are due to disloyalty, idleness, cowardice, untidiness, lack of concentration and lack of care. The faults, in other words, are more moral than intellectual; and moral qualities vary from day to day, being governed by external influences, of which leadership is the chief. There are no bad troops, it is said; only bad officers. In the world of industry and commerce, the morale of the work force is something built up by company policy but it is not uninfluenced by the general conditions of boom or slump, nor again by a variety of local circumstances which include the commuting problem and do not exclude the weather. Some human characteristics, like intelligence, are plainly hereditary but the basic requirement for efficiency—a reluctance to go home until the job is properly done—is as variable as the wind. We know this from our own example, with our energy almost feverish at one time and almost non-existent at another. There remains, it is true, a typical level for any given person but it may rise steeply at the prospect of promotion and fall as dramatically at the prospect of retirement.

The fixed ceiling of competence is a myth, as has been proved repeatedly in time of revolution. Another myth is the belief that everyone works for promotion until the point is reached where all further promotion is denied. People with effective ambition are in fact relatively few. Some would take higher office were it given them but a majority would be embarrassed by the offer. Were we on the bridge of *Queen Elizabeth II* in New York harbour, we should not, most of us, be overjoyed were the captain to say, 'All right—*you* take her to sea!' Our mental picture at that moment would not be one of personal triumph but of imminent disaster, with the destruction of the Statue of Liberty a mere incident in the subsequent sequence of sad surprises. The number of boys who say that their object in life is to become President of the United States is probably quite small. After some explanation is given of all that this post will entail, the number must dwindle to almost nothing. That the occupant of the office will prove incompetent is highly probable—the duties being far beyond what is reasonable—but this is no proof of the Peter Principle. For the applicants were few and the one finally chosen has not, of necessity, proved conspicuously competent as (say) the governor of a state.

It is doubtful, finally, whether the majority of promotions— even at a lower than presidential level—are governed by the candidate's competence as shown on the rung below. In most organizations a barrier exists which the majority of employees can never surmount. In some offices the higher posts go only to relatives of the chairman, in others only to graduates of Princeton. For success in Corporation A you must be a White Anglo-Saxon Protestant, (WASP). For success in Corporation B you must be a Developing Region Off-White Neurotic Episcopalian (DRONE), while nobody can reach the Board of Corporation C who is not a Southern Typically Opinionated Irish Catholic (STOIC). It is manifest, as Dr. Peter himself admits, that the existence of such a barrier will keep some people to a level below their ceiling—even supposing that they have a ceiling—and that others may be promoted on grounds which have nothing to do with competence. Even, moreover, in organizations which theoretically offer the same prospects to everyone, the competence which gains the highest reward may be quite unrelated to the work in hand. A successful career may be founded on a competence in passing examinations, furthered by a competence in flattery and crowned by a competence in marrying into the right family. Each type of competence is real enough but is not strictly comparable with the sorts of competence in which rival executives may have specialized. From even the most casual observation we can fairly conclude that Peter's Principle is not applicable to public or business administration nor to any of the hierarchies which are concerned with trade or war. It is a factor only in the world of education and more particularly in the sector of that world which is concerned with educationalization. Even in that sector it may not be universal but may apply mainly to Southern California. One may suspect, indeed, that Peter's Principle holds good only in the Excelsior City School System. The Kingdom of Incompetence may turn out to be as small as that, with only this one Peter to hold the keys.

CHAPTER 8

From Hand to Mouth

Speech serves two purposes. The older and basic object is to express an emotion, unburdening the mind of its immediate content. The later and more sophisticated object is to convey a message to someone else. Older than speech, however, and similarly divided in aim, is the language of gesture, shared by man with other animals. Men without a common spoken language can communicate, up to a point, as animals do. By grimace and pantomime they can easily express their more elemental reactions of surprise, annoyance, affection, impatience, desire and grief.

With more difficulty, and with more risk of ambiguity, they can even convey a simple message—one of hostility, for example, of warning, of welcome or rejection. As compared with other animals, apes accepted, man had more scope for gesture as from the time he ceased to be four-legged. By standing up, he left his hands free to signal, the message being further underlined, on occasion, by expressions of the face of movements of the head. Movements of the foot are, of course, older still, deriving from the four-legged pre-ape ancestors. A horse's pawing of the ground, as a sign of impatience, is a gesture which human beings have retained in a modified form. To stamp with rage must be among the oldest gestures; more expressive of emotion, however, than of any desire to communicate. It is significant that emotions are often registered without anyone else being present. We relieve our feelings by a gesture of which there is no other witness, proving that we have nothing useful to convey.

The language of gesture, shared by man with other animals

Speech came later to mankind. It enables us to express more complex emotions and allows us to convey messages that are more detailed and precise. But the gift of speech is enjoyed very unequally among different racial, cultural and intellectual groups. The language of a Malay peasant or Arab tribesman may be very elementary. That of a German philosopher may be elaborate to the point of obscurity. What seems odd is that this development of language has not led to the abandonment of gesture. The world is full of people whose every remark has to be underlined by a gesture. They cannot say, 'I don't know,' without shrugging their shoulders. They never say 'Yes' without nodding the head. In a few instances the gesture is effective, a deliberate emphasis of a particular point. On far more occasions the gesture is a futile repetition of what has been said.

Why do we have to gesticulate? In attempting to answer this question we must first observe how people behave when using the telephone. Watching through the glass of a public phone booth, we can often see what is virtually a pantomime performance. The caller's expression changes from one of concern to one of delight. The hand waves with excitement or disapproval. The finger points in this direction or that. The shoulders shrug in gloomy acceptance and the feet tap with impatience and disgust.

All these gestures are made into a blind receiver which seems to prove that they are an end in themselves, not meant as a message to anyone else. They are used merely as an outlet for emotions which the caller can no longer contain. The person who merely wants to babble for a given period of time is unable, as a rule, to imagine the effect of what he or she has to say. It does not cross her mind (or his) that the person at the other end of the line may be uninterested, bored or cross, with troubles of her own and with work which has to be done. She may not even realize that her friend's receiver has been laid down while the theoretical recipient of her confidences has gone off to answer the door or feed the cat. Her whole attention is concentrated, in fact, on herself, her basic lack of imagination being proved by her use of gesture. That people will smile or frown at a receiver (which, visually, receives nothing) is a human habit of which we may be generally aware. That it reveals, above all, a lack of imagination may be less widely known; and yet the fact would seem to be obvious.

The telephone babbler has so far been assumed to be female because the housewife suffers more from isolation, but men can be almost equally unimaginative. Watch, for example, a host who is directing, on the telephone, a couple who have failed to find their way to the cocktail party. 'Where are you now, then?. . . Opposite the Public Library?. . . Well, it's perfectly simple from there. Go on until you come to the Town Hall, where the road forks. Bear left there (gesture) and drive for about a mile until you reach a new department block on your left (gesture). Turn (gesture) just beyond it and then take the second (gesture) turning to the right (gesture). That is Sycamore Street, a cul-de-sac and ours is the very end house on the left (gesture). Got it? That's fine then. We'll see you in about ten minutes.' But *will* the guests be there so soon? The weakness of this directive lies in the fact that the host is waving his hand about instead of concentrating on verbal precision. In this instance he has omitted an essential word, relying upon a gesture which his guests cannot see. There is the further possibility that he has said 'left' at some other point where he should have said 'right'. Passers-by often do that when asked the way and they frequently point at the same time in the other direction. When this occurs we know from experience that the gesture will be correct and that the word will be wrong. Over the telephone, however, the word flies on its way uncorrected by its visual counterpart.

Still more misleading is the indoor directive, as when Professor X tells a student where to find (in Castle Y) the little-known portrait of Archbishop W, which is usually, if doubtfully, attributed to the artist Z. 'You cross the second courtyard, go down the steps and bear right. Go up the spiral staircase (corkscrew gesture) and you will find yourself in the Armoury. To the left (gesture right) of the fireplace there is a door which leads into the Tapestry Room, from which another staircase (gesture, spiral upward) leads you to the Muniment Room—originally a chapel—and there (gesture upwards, left) you will find the picture. It is about this size (gesture) and must not be confused with a rather similar portrait on the opposite (gesture, right) side of the room.' In this sort of attempted description the speaker cannot, apparently, put himself in the place of the person he is trying to direct. To do that would require an effort of imagination of which the professor, we must suppose, is incapable. Our criticism of the hand-waving habit is based not merely on the fact that it argues a poverty of language but that it is allowed to take the place of words which ought to have been uttered. Gesticulating at a receiver is only slightly more absurd than gesticulating in ordinary conversation. If we would only pay attention to what we are saying, our words should be enough to convey what we mean.

In general we might dare to conclude that people who gesticulate most freely are those, more often, with emotions to register, less frequently those with a message to convey. Observation might also incline us to believe that gestures are used more by women than men—more by latins than by teutons—more by the illiterate than by the educated—more by the young than by the old.

Such generalizations may be open to question but the use of gesture would seem, at first sight, to indicate a poor vocabulary and becomes most universal, perhaps, when the needed word escapes us. In varying degrees then there is a widespread human tendency to say everything twice. The later speech is reinforced by the earlier, and usually redundant, gesture. It would make sense if half of us were deaf but otherwise it seems absurd.

Where emotions are concerned there may be the satisfaction of added emphasis (although the effect on others must be weakened through mere repetition). But on the whole, the instances are few in which the gesture is advisable and fewer still in which it is needed. There is a case against gesticulating at all and it is based on the assumption that grimaces and hand wavings are the resort of the mentally lazy. Take the occasion when our message may have been understood, but when we have failed to convey it by words alone. The result may be that out next attempt at verbal communication may fail. Unused to mental effort, our imagination stunted by our habitual failure to appreciate anyone else's point of view, we may well gesticulate where speech is vital—in the dark, for example, or on the telephone.

Our conclusion must be that the deliberate and possibly rehearsed gesture, as used by an orator or actor, can be effective and can even be needed as emphasis. We may recall further instances in which words fail us and in which a gesture may be essential to complete the sense of what we are trying to say. Beyond this allowable or unavoidable usage, however, we should discourage gesticulation—in the young, for example—as a proof of mental sloth. Where we fall back on grimace and gesture it is not because the language fails us but because we have failed to learn all that it has to offer. The remedy is to read widely, think deeply, talk less and listen more.

If the gestures made by the individual are the relic of some more primitive age, no proof in themselves of imagination or ability, what are we to make of group gestures and mob uproar? We may suspect that the planned demonstration is something peculiar to this age, a daily degradation unknown before this century began. Such a suspicion would be unfounded, the novelty lying not in the public gesture but in the television programme which is what the organizers of the riot are seeking to secure. That disorders are thus caused by the television camera is a sad comment on our way of life. Having admitted as much, we must still deplore the current fashion for shuffling through the streets in support of this cause or in condemnation of that. The procession may have a goal, an embassy to be stoned, a meeting to be interrupted, a protest to be made. It may often lead from nowhere to nowhere, proving no more than that so many people have views about a particular issue.

But whether law-abiding or violent, the demonstrators have shown their preference for the gesture, their disdain for the written word. With clenched fists or arm upraised, with shouted slogan or implied threat, the mob turns aside from coherent speech and reverts to the gibbering of the apes. There is little the mob member does which a gorilla could not do as well or better. With mob behaviour and gesture we are fairly back in the Stone Age, having agreed to reject all that has since been achieved. The fist-shaking mobster is neither citizen nor soldier, neither thinker nor artist, lower than a sheepdog and far less than a man. If there is something short of the adult in the individual grimace, its primitive origin becomes apparent in its multiplied caricature. The demonstrator's mindless hysteria is a denial of civilization.

The time has come, then, to look at gesture again. For if the demonstration in the street (a gesture shared with others) is a long step back towards the Stone Age, we may be justified in our suspicion that the gestures made by the individual are a relic of some more primitive period and no proof, in themselves, of intelligence or education. Let us look again at the panel members who appear on the television screen. Do their gestures serve any purpose? Do wavings of the hand complete a meaning or lend emphasis to an argument? Or do they merely weary us by pointless repetition? Graduates of the drama school may be able to show how the gestures rehearsed may serve to reveal the character or further the plot. Granted that this is so, can the same be said of the gestures made by those who have had no special training on the stage or in the court of law? The effectiveness of the trial lawyer's thump on the table depends upon the rarity of the gesture and its timing, for the trick used too often may rather seem to weaken the argument. Compare with that the fidgets which afflict the televised talker. Study, finally, the videotape of our own performance. Watch the facial expression, the eyebrows lowered, the shoulders shrugged and the forefinger raised. Which gesture served a purpose? What was the effect of those other gestures, which merely reflected an inability to sit still? They may have revealed your character but is that the aspect of your character which you wish to reveal? Did they persuade, those gestures, or did they rather distract? Did they emphasize or did they merely irritate? Let us begin to watch now with a more critical eye and with a new determination to make better use of the gift of speech, which is peculiar to man, and to minimize the use of gesture which we have in common with the apes. Let us decide rather to concentrate upon the right use of our noble language, the tongue developed and enriched by Shakespeare and Milton, by Newton and Johnson, by Jefferson and Lincoln. In the words of the prayer book, keep our tongue from lying and slandering and our hands from picking, stealing and (incidentally) fidgeting. So shall we learn to mean what we say, and—eventually, perhaps—to say what we mean.

CHAPTER 9

Left is Right

Many people throughout the world were shocked and indeed appalled by the undemocratic and retrogressive way in which Sweden (in 1967) reversed its ancient rule of the road, reducing by one the number of countries in which vehicles keep to the left. In this matter only a handful of countries still confront and oppose the Soviet-American bloc. There are folk who regard this question as a matter of indifference or as a debate to be settled by mere weight of numbers. As in the parallel case of centimetres, hectares, litres and grams, there is more, however, to the controversy than meets the eye. It is not a matter in which those outvoted should gracefully concede defeat. It is a matter, rather, in which great moral principles are at stake. We should be prepared to fight for our beliefs, if necessary for years and if necessary alone. We must let it be known throughout the civilized world that might, in this context, is not right. This is an instance, rather of left being right and of right being wrong.

The ancient custom of riding or driving on the left of the road is founded upon some of the deepest known instincts. It is quite false to suppose that this is a matter of indifference to be settled by the whim of an ignorant majority. The human body itself has its own bias from the outset, the heart being placed (or appearing to be placed) on the left. Upon this basic fact rests the first principle of tactics in personal combat, which is to attack with the right hand while protecting the heart with the left. When the stick or cudgel turned eventually into the sword, it was soon discovered that a weapon of any but the shortest length, if used in the right hand, must be worn on the left hip. The scabbard comes thus to its natural position and would impose a severe handicap if worn in any other fashion.

With the scabbard on the left, the warrior's next problem, at a later period of history, was how to mount his horse. Repeated and often disastrous experiment led him to the conclusion that the wearer of a sword has to mount on the left (a contrary policy must leave him facing the horse's tail). In addition, the horse is naturally mounted while standing on the left side of the road. The rider is thus less exposed to the passing traffic and once there, had better stay there. Should the horseman carry a lance, he has additional reasons for keeping to the left: the reduced likelihood of entanglement with overhanging branches and the readier threat to any opponent who might approach from the opposite direction.

Supplant the horseman by a wheeled vehicle and the case becomes stronger still. For the coachman, still right-handed, will have reins collected in his left, leaving the whip in his right. Given a team of four or more, the driver needs space on his right, without which he cannot touch the flanks of his leading horse. To make that space he must keep in to the left, as he must always have done. He would thus have the whip hand of any rival who sought to overtake him on the right. For the waggon, for the coach or cabriolet, the left was certainly preferable. It is for good, sound and basic reasons that the traffic of more civilized countries has always kept to that side.

But the logic which brings the vehicle to the left is not equally applicable to the pedestrian. For while his primitive instinct must take him to the left, as it still does, one notices, in entering a store or restaurant—a later development had the opposite effect. Given a sword or pistol, the duellist presents his right side to an opponent, at once minimizing the target and protecting the heart. But give him a shield and his motives are reversed. He will then present his

The rider is thus less exposed to the passing traffic

left side foremost so as to make fullest use of the shield, his right or attacking arm being held initially in reserve.

The medieval infantryman edged therefore to the right, a fact which came to be reflected in the architecture of the time. In the medieval castle the winding staircase was usually given a clockwise twist from the bottom. Given the situation of a last desperate stand, with defenders retreating to the upper floor, the assaulting soldier thus found his shield useless against the outer wall and his sword arm severely hampered. The pedestrian has some historical reason, therefore, for keeping to the right—however much his innate instincts would keep him to the left.

In this last circumstance there might seem to be some slight justification for the extraordinary customs observed on the American highways. But such an idea would be baseless. The fact is that pedestians *should* keep to the right of any thoroughfare in which the vehicles are keeping to the left. They are thus able to see what is coming. Vehicles have to meet them face to face; they cannot as readily sneak up behind, stalking them and wriggling into a position from which to pounce. The British are always more concerned about horses (or dogs) than about human beings, and it was they who insisted, as recently as 1930, that anyone leading an animal must not only keep to the right but must place himself between it and the traffic—remembering that men are expendable but that horses are not.

In the face of all these unanswerable arguments for keeping to the left, it must seem odd indeed that the opposite custom should prevail in some countries which are only moderately backward in other respects. How is it that Britain and Sweden retained the medieval rule of the road when the French and their satellites adopted the opposite plan, as a sequel, presumably, to the French Revolution? Why, indeed, should the change have been made?

It was clearly an instance of innovation for its own sake and may well have coincided with other nonsensical legislation affecting the calendar, the decimal system, weights and measures, provincial boundaries and heaven knows what else. The inconvenience of the republican calendar was perceived almost from the first. The disadvantages of the decimal system are at least as apparent today (mathematicians recognizing that the duodecimal system is preferable). But this driving on the right has been maintained with persistence, and has even been extended, since 1815.

To this trend, Britain eventually replied with Section 78 of the Highways Act of 1853. Until that year the rule of the road had been a matter of common law of an antiquity too remote for anything but conjecture. Thenceforward it had statutory authority, being expressly applied to motor vehicles in 1904. In wisdom the Highways Act ranks second only to the law which provided that any horseless carriage should be preceded by someone on foot carrying a red flag; a law which, steadfastly enforced, would have saved us heavy casualties and expense. Its repeal in 1896 was a major disaster, leading of necessity to an outcry about making roads suitable for motor vehicles. While such roads are admittedly more under discussion than construction in Britain, there can be no doubt that they will become, when made, a needless burden. With the advent, however, of the private hovercraft or helicopter, the British may well shelve the whole problem and proceed to the next.

The reasoning which is so conclusive as applied to the land is by no means applicable to the sea. For here the traffic consists not of vehicles but of ships. And ships are governed by other circumstances; more especially by a feature of their original design. The medieval ship inherited from Scandinavia a steering oar which projected from the steering-board, steerboard or starboard side. Meeting in a narrow waterway, two medieval ships did well to avoid splintering their steering oars, which they could easily provide against by keeping to the right, or starboard, side of the channel. This they did and the custom has been retained.

It must be admitted, however, that this contrast between the rules of the road as observed ashore and afloat does give rise to some possible difficulty. Sir Alan Herbert drew attention to this in his Misleading Cases of the Common Law, putting the problem of what is to happen in shallow water when a vehicle meets a boat? In the special case cited, the Thames had flooded its banks and the plaintiff, driving a car, sustained damage in seeking to avoid collision with the defendant's canoe. The plaintiff was able to show that he had kept to the left. The defendant was prepared to swear that he had kept to starboard. Nor were the facts even in dispute. The case turned rather upon the definition of the terms 'tideway' and 'navigable water'. Was the Thames embankment a part of the river, when flooded, and so under admiralty jurisdiction? Would a hold-up in the same place, and at the same state of the tide, have constituted an act of piracy? Questions such as these, fascinating as they may be, are not to the present purpose. Whatever their complexities and however they may be settled, the fact remains that such incidents are unlikely to occur. Whatever the theoretical risk of having opposite rules for sea and land, the practical dangers would seem to be negligible.

Ancient custom being thus justified by physiological, historical and logical reasoning, it must seem very strange that a British Minister of Transport should have called for a report on the implications of Britain changing its rule of the road. To call for a report and to accept its conclusions are not, admittedly, the same thing. The fact remains, however, that some serious consideration is being given to the proposal—a fact disturbing in itself. That the change will be infinitely postponed in view of its appalling expense may perhaps be assumed. But opponents of the scheme have dwelt mainly on the cost of changing traffic lights and reversing vehicle designs, failing to arouse, as they should have done, the natural and-proper resentment felt by the British toward any foreign interference. The success of a Napoleon or Hitler would have led to this very innovation, a single aspect of the continental tyrannies which Britain has consistently opposed. The fact is that driving on the right is, frankly, not playing the game. This is especially apparent when we study the circular traffic intersection known colloquially as a 'roundabout'. It contrasts favourably with the fly-over, a device used elsewhere to minimize the sporting chance. But the point to notice is that the British user of a 'roundabout' is revolving clockwise. To reverse the movement, going 'widdershins' against the sun and against all decent observance in circulating the after-dinner wine, would be most unlucky.

The question, finally, is not whether Britain will follow the example of Russia, but whether, and when, other less civilized countries will fall into line with Britain. Some impatience has been shown with the French, for example, whose obstinacy in this matter is proverbial. It is a question, however, whether uniformities of custom are a real advantage. Our pleasure in travel derives from the fact that other peoples are not the same, but different. We do better, therefore, to encourage foreigners to retain their own quaint traditions.

If there is a case for bringing pressure to bear on France, it must result from the projected tunnel or bridge which is to link Britain with the Continent. What is to happen halfway if the French refuse to conform? Much has been made of this difficulty but is it really so serious? It would be no great matter, surely, to transpose the traffic streams at the midway point, the one swooping below the other to appear next minute on the other side. Would not this device relieve the monotony of an otherwise tedious drive? As for the French railways, the difficulty does not arise. They were originally planned by a British engineer and one who would stand no nonsense from the natives. The French railways have held, from the beginning, to the left.

CHAPTER 10

Revolting Youth

In September, 1969, a crowd of young people, perhaps two hundred in number, occupied an old town house at Hyde Park Corner in the very centre of London, being finally thrown out of it by the police. The incident attracted a great deal of publicity, as it was meant to do, but less attention was paid to the same group's previous occupation of another building forming a part of Charing Cross Hospital. When the intruders had gone the building was in such a state that a hospital official, inspecting it, was physically sick and a policewoman collapsed and was carried out. These incidents were reported and also served to inspire a number of articles in which leading journalists discussed the problem of youth in revolt. One newspaper, going further, published a useful analysis of the problem as it affected London at that time. According to this report[1] our capital city then contained three main groups of rebellious youth—the Hippies, the Skinheads, and Hell's Angels. The respective numbers of these for Britain as a whole would have been, by this estimate and at that time, sixty thousand, seven thousand five hundred, and two thousand. Dissimilar in many ways and hostile towards each other, these groups were at least alike in rebellion. Adding smaller groups to the total we might conclude that Britain had at that time about seventy-five thousand young rebels out of its population of fifty-five million.

These figures for 1969 were only approximate and we must

[1] *Daily Mail*, 26 September 1969.

suppose that the picture has changed since then, groups vanishing and re-forming, names being changed, some growing up and others reaching adolescence. We might guess, however, that the total has not dramatically increased or diminished. As against that we have to recognize that the total number, whatever it is, must be deceptive. For every full-time hippy there are ten other youngsters who are in some degree under hippy influence. Hell's Angels do what a far larger number would like to do. They at once represent and influence a high proportion of the young. Their doings are reported and admired and their style of dress is partly copied. Where they have taken violent action they have seldom been effectively opposed by non-members of their organization. It is significant that many of the young have ceased to imitate heroes of the older generation—even the space travellers—and prefer to emulate their own heroes—pop singers and drug addicts. So our problem in Britain is not with seventy-five thousand or a hundred thousand rebels against convention but with a far larger number of those who have not been immune to their influence. We have also to realize that our problem, whatever its origin, is as familiar to the central and local authorities of Germany, France and Holland. Our problem lies in the reluctance of the young, or of some of them, to enter society as it exists, and this trend is found in a number of countries today, U.S.A. being one of them and Japan another.

While this difficulty with the young is common, it is not universal. For in societies which are still based on agriculture the authority of age is still fairly secure. Youth would seem to rebel more readily in a technically advanced and advancing society in which the old have lost their advantage, their traditional wisdom having come to be regarded as obsolescence. The situation is probably reached in two distinct steps. The effect of industrialism is, first of all, to weaken and eventually destroy the human family as a working unit. The extended family of up to four generations is scattered and we are left with the small nucleus comprising only parents and children, often with the mother at work. It may take up to fifty years to kill the family but in many areas this has now been done. The second step is to progress in such a way that the young man, fresh from a computer course, is better qualified than an older man whose longer experience is now thought to be useless. The American organization which has placed astronauts on the moon has thus its own status system, based not on seniority but on the number of doors which each member is entitled to pass. Our Beatniks and Hippies have no knowledge of electronics (or of anything else) but they have absorbed the idea that the elderly have lost their prestige. Their background is essentially industrial.

The problem of youth in revolt begins with the generation which just missed service in World War II. This was the 'Beat' or 'Beaten' generation, born in about 1928–9, which includes, for example, John Osborne, the British dramatist. Members of this age group were disillusioned by the fact that the Hot War begun by Germany was promptly followed by the Cold War between Russia and U.S.A. Their views were well expressed by an American novelist, Jack Kerouac (born in Canada, 1922) whose first book was published in 1950. A similar attitude to life was expressed by Marlon Brando in a motion picture called *The Wild Ones*. Members of the same 'Beat' generation were the Teddy Boys of Britain. Most of the young people, however, who were disillusioned by the aftermath of World War II held socialist views and looked to Russia for salvation. That last illusion went with the attempted Hungarian revolution of 1956. That event was proof in their eyes that Soviet Russia was no better than U.S.A. and quite as ruthless in pursuing its own interests. More significant books appeared in 1957 and 1958 and the Russian 'Sputnik' or space rocket of 1959 gave rise to the term 'Beatnik', a variant of the older word 'Beat'. It is thus a dozen years or more since the movement for rejecting society took shape. Since then the names have changed, the Beatniks giving place to the Mods and Rockers and these again to the Hippies and Skinheads, to the Bodgies of Australia and the Provos of Holland.

So far as the Beatniks were concerned their largest concentration was in California, the State which represents the ultimate in American progress and sophistication. Migrants to California came largely from the other States in the Union, this final move involving a second, third or fourth uprooting. Remote now from every family tie, the migrants have come west and further west, seeking the sunshine and moving to areas in which the main industries are the latest. The agricultural traditions were left behind with great-grandparents in New England or Poland. Ideas associated with heavy industry were left behind with grandparents in the Middle West. All that is latest and best, all that is progressive and enlightened will be found in California. And if there is one place in California which contains the essence of all that is most enlightened it is, beyond question, the Berkeley campus of the State University. To reject Berkeley is to reject California. To reject California is to reject U.S.A. To reject U.S.A. is to reject the entire western world, if not the world itself. And that was exactly what happened. A group of university students rejected not what older people might deplore but the very centre upon which national pride should concentrate. From the hippy quarter of San Francisco a movement of revolt spread to Berkeley, taking the form of demonstrations, disorder and riot. From there it spread to other universities, affecting places as remote from each other as London, Frankfurt, Amsterdam, Paris and Tokyo. The moment began, however, in the main academic centre of the most attractive city in the most prosperous State of the world's leading Nation.

Student demonstrations have since become so common that they are accepted now as a matter of course, a natural outlet for emotion. What few seem to realize is that a demonstration—whatever its object—is a denial of everything for which a university stands. The first principle of scholarship, established by Socrates and upheld by Aristotle, is the student's admission of ignorance. We enter a university because we do not know, because we want to learn. Our views, if we have any, are to be tested by the light of reason. Our opinions, when we acquire them, are to be supported by an application of logic to facts which we are prepared to prove. No scholar in the world will shuffle through the streets, carrying a banner and shouting a slogan. Why not? Because reiteration, noise and threats are no part of academic life. Nothing becomes more true because we shout it repeatedly and loudly. Nothing even becomes more true because people vote for it. Tell a workman or schoolteacher that the earth is flat and he will probably answer 'Rubbish!'. Make the same remark to a scholar and he will probably ask 'How do you *know*?' He may be interested in a possible line of argument. Socrates, the very founder of the academic way of life, seems never to have made any dogmatic assertions about anything. Pleading ignorance, he merely asked questions. We who have sought to follow in his path are as little likely to shout each other down.

Persons are to be seen carrying placards which read 'Yankee imperialists—quit Vietnam!' Some among them may be registered as students of a university but they have been admitted in error and should be expelled at once, not for the criminal offence of causing a riot but for the academic offence of regarding reiteration as proof. A real student, one rightly admitted, might express his tentative opinion in some such words as these: 'So far as I understand the facts, I incline to question whether the Americans have much to gain by keeping armed forces at their present strength in Vietnam.' Scholars have many weaknesses and faults but they still retain the central truth of their creed, which might be worded thus: 'The slogan shouted a thousand times each by ten thousand believers is no more likely to be true than the opposite belief voiced once in a whisper by one.' That is the first step towards scholarship and we make no progress until that step has been taken.

The student revolution at Berkeley took place in 1964 and ended with the resignation of the university's president, a very distinguished man. If we ask at this point why such a movement should succeed and spread, we have to ask the wider question 'How does *any* revolt spread?' The answer must be that men never revolt against tyranny but always against an authority which weakens and wavers. It is not a characteristic of mankind to hurl itself against a door that is locked and bolted. The push comes against the door which stands ajar; against the flimsy door with a broken lock. The story of any revolution begins not with the conspiracy of the rebels but with dissension and doubt among the men in office. It is the decay of government which creates the vacuum into which the rebellion is drawn. Faced with the revolt of youth we should ask, first of all, what guilt complex, what weakness, is to be observed among the adult? For of this we can be certain, that the men and women who are fully grown have every means at hand with which to suppress or at least contain the revolt of youth. Nothing could be simpler or easier. The first weapon, and the most potent, is the power to ignore it. If all the television and radio commentators agreed with all the journalists—adults agreeing with adults—to give no coverage to any youth demonstration for any object, the movement would slow down. The second weapon, to supplement the first, is the power of ridicule. The third weapon is that of infiltration and there are several others, some more severe. If these and other weapons are not used it is because we, the elderly, feel vulnerable and guilty. We ask each other whether we are to blame, whether we should not have called the young into consultation, whether there should not be younger men in power, whether people should not have the vote at eighteen, at sixteen, at ten. If we ask how the movement succeeds and spreads the answer is clear: it is spread by us.

The movement of rebellious youth is cultivated and encouraged by those who are no longer young. The fact remains, however, that the movement has very unequal success in this society as opposed to that. We have noted that respect for age goes with agriculture and that rebellion seems to go with the more advanced type of industry. But what is it in a technically advanced society that is repulsive to some of the young? Conversely we may ask what factor it is in other societies, or in our own society at a different period, which provides the magnetism, which holds people together? The fact is, surely, that the magnetism of a society—that which attracts everyone, the young included—is created by its momentum. The countries which have had the most powerful attractions have been those committed to the greatest external tasks. In Austria and Poland the task was once to save Europe from the threat of Islam. In Spain the task was once to explore and develop the New World. The object in France was to grasp and retain the leadership of Europe. The object in U.S.A. was once to colonize North America just as the object in Russia was to colonize Central Asia. In Britain our object was once to govern and develop the British Empire overseas. In all these and many other instances the adults could turn to the young and say 'Help us to do what has to be done. The work is exhausting and dangerous. We need your help.' The magnetism of a society lies in just that sort of appeal and that is the tremendous strength of the communist countries. In U.S.A. those in authority say to the young. 'Look what we offer you! You have school, college, culture and sport, with colour television, travel and counselling. What more can you want?' What they want is a goal. The marching column which people want to join is one which appears to be going somewhere; and this is a fact which the communists have perceived. They make no promises of comfort, they merely demand recruits for a dangerous mission. That appeal is strong, especially to the sort of recruits who are worth recruiting.

If we are to regain the loyalty of the young who stray we must offer them some object external to the society in which they are to live. Socialism is not enough and is mostly in fact irrelevant. It is the aim of our reformers to make people more safe and prosperous, with special emphasis on care for the sick and the old. These might be useful by-products of a general campaign but what we lack is the campaign itself. What, in non-material terms, are we

The marching column which people want to join is the one which appears
to be going somewhere

trying to do? To this question the marxists have an answer, and even one as obsolete as theirs is better perhaps than none. What is our answer to be? Until we can answer that question our society will lack any magnetic attraction for youth. But we should be utterly wrong to suppose that a number of countries can or should have the same aim. It is far more likely that most of them will have a different task —if only, like Israel, the task of survival.

For Britain, it would seem, the mission must be to disband the Commonwealth and fit itself into the community of Europe. To perform this feat will require a tremendous effort of imagination, of perception, of adaptability and skill. We have to grasp, first of all, that foolish attempts to copy our new partners (substituting kilometres for miles) are beside the point. Our need is rather to revise our approach to geography and history, striving first and foremost to make Europe a reality; a substitute, moreover, for what we have lost. Scandinavia offers us an example of what can be done. They have already formed there a group of four countries between which there are no rigid frontiers, no need for passports. That, surely, is what the future holds for us; the experience of being in Holland or Austria combined with the sense of being still at home. In a peaceful and creative sense, we have worlds to conquer. The time has come for us to set about it.

CHAPTER 11

On Humour

Britain's contribution to the civilized world must include the British sense of humour; which means, incidentally, the British sense of proportion. There are solemn people who will deny the importance of humour, questioning whether a mere joke can serve any useful purpose. In this, their attitude, the solemn folk are totally mistaken. The joke can serve several purposes, some not merely useful but essential. It can be the means of memorizing a lesson, one which would otherwise be forgotten. It can be the means of relieving tension, as when a joke prevents a massacre. It can be the means, finally, of making a distinction between the vital and the trivial. There should be room in the world for humour and we do well to consider its function and scope. We also do well to remember that anyone can be solemn but that one needs intelligence to be funny. The court jester was once the holder of a public office, reminding statesmen that there might be, on any issue, another point of view. Such a reminder is still of value and the jester's career is not in vain.

The jokes available to us are basically four in number, as follows: the Homeric Joke, the Disappointed Joke, the Joke about Sex and the Joke about Words. The Homeric Joke is the oldest and simplest. It concerns the mishap which results from a physical or moral defect, blindness, deafness, intoxication, clumsiness or cowardice. In this primary joke, as exemplified in the works of Homer, the King or Chief Priest strides majestically into the meeting, trips over the doormat and falls on his nose. We still use that joke on television and any child will enjoy it as an incident in pantomime. Cowardice is always a good subject for humour, provided only that the coward has some pretence to courage, as in wearing a uniform. The negro, on joining the army, is asked whether he would like to serve in the cavalry. 'No, sir,' he replies. 'When that thar trumpet sounds the retreat, I don't want to be hampered by no horse.' This is a physical type of joke, our mental picture being one of the negro in flight. In its more sophisticated form, however, the mishap can be verbal rather than physical. In *Punch*, of many years ago, the picture is thus shown of a very important man descending the steps of a London Club in immaculate evening dress with white tie, opera cloak and hat. In the foreground two taxi drivers are in conversation and one turns to the other and says, 'Bill, 'ave you ever 'eard of Gawd?' Bill admits that he has and the first driver says, 'Well, that's 'is brother, Archibald.' This is, as it were, the verbal equivalent of a banana skin under the impressive Club member's feet. The same joke is implicit in the old rhyme which went:

> He was really as mild as a lamb,
> Until he sat down on the jam,
> When taking his seat
> At the Sunday School Treat
> The Vicar distinctly said. . . . 'And now children, if
> you'll all stand up we will say grace.'

Two elements are essential to the complete success of the joke. The first is that the King or Bishop must be really venerated. The fall of someone unimportant or the expected fall of a drunkard would not have the same impact. The second element is that the fall must not lead to serious injury or death. There is a laughable inconsistency between a high office in society and a prone position on the doorstep. There is no inconsistency between kingship and death. Given a fatal injury the incident ceases to be funny.

The world's second joke is concerned with disappointment, the contrast between what we expect and what we find. Guests arrive for a banquet which took place the day before. The crowd assembles to watch a cricket match only to find the pitch flooded. The expression on the face of the enthusiasts is amusing to those who have no interest in the game. The bridegroom appears at the well-decorated church in proper attire and with numerous relatives, but there is no bride. Whether she has been abducted or whether she is waiting at another church, the bridegroom's air of frustration may amuse the choirboys and bystanders. In a television play a new ambassador is being ceremoniously received at the airport. Walking into the smoke belched from the ancient saluting cannon, he misses the reception group, advancing past them with hand outstretched while his hosts do the same in the opposite direction. This joke is the better for including elements also of the first or primary joke, represented in this instance by his white uniform, decorations, plumed hat and sword.

The world's third joke is about sex. In most human societies there is an accepted pattern of sex relationships. Marriage, for example, is a legal institution with wives numbering from one to four. Wives may be assumed to be virgin until married. Men expect to dominate the sex partnership and wives do well to obey. The pattern may vary but the pattern exists. Jokes then centre upon the variants; the man with a mistress as well as a wife, the wife with a milkman as well as a husband, the man who is effeminate and the wife who is not. Jokes about the husband's excuses for being out late are as numerous as jokes about the wife's lover hidden under the bed. The elderly barrister comes home unexpectedly to find another man in bed with his young wife. His resentment seems to her absurd. 'But, really, dear,' she asks afterwards, 'were you *surprised*?' But her husband chooses his words more carefully. 'No,' he says. '*You* were surprised, *I* was astounded.' It must be admitted, however, that this story includes an element of the world's fourth joke. Purer in type, if not in content, is the story of

The world's third joke is about sex

the bride who was asked, before the wedding, what sort of cere-
mony she approved. 'Do you like big weddings,' the bridegroom
asked, 'or little ones?' She considered the matter carefully and then
replied, 'I think mummy and daddy would be happier if I had the
big wedding *first.*' An even simpler joke concerns the Polish airman undergoing a psychology test. 'Suppose,' said the psychologist, 'that you are at the stern of a ship, looking down into
the swirling turbulence made by the propeller. What does it make
you think of?' 'Sex,' said the airman promptly. The psychologist,
used to men who replied, 'A pint of beer,' was frankly puzzled.
'Sex?' he repeated, 'Why on earth should you think of *sex?*' 'Because I never think of anything else.'

   The world's fourth joke is purely verbal, a joke which centres
upon the ambiguous, unusual or mistaken use of words—as, for
example, in mistranslation, mispronunciation or misspelling. The
foreigner's mistaken use of words is thus exemplified in the story
of the French visitor to England who was asked whether he had
any children. He shook his head sadly but felt that some explana-
tion was due. 'Unfortunately,' he said, 'my wife is unbearable.' He
sensed that he had used the wrong word and quickly corrected
himself. 'I mean,' he added, 'that my wife is impregnable.' He
felt again that he had given the wrong impression and tried once
more. 'I should have said,' he went on desperately, 'that my wife
is inconceivable.' The humour of words extends to the spoonerism
and the pun. It was Dr. Spooner who is said to have misplaced his
syllables as in rebuking a student with the words: 'You have hissed
my mystery lectures—in fact, you have tasted a whole worm.'
As for the pun, it probably reaches perfection in the story of the
anarchist who went to the Spanish bullfight. Cad that he was, he
threw a bomb into the arena. The bull saw the bomb and swal-
lowed it and all the crowd shouted, 'Abominable!' Similar in type
of humour is the poem about the soldier who left on the battlefield
his second leg and the twenty-second foot. Similar again is the
logicians' old syllogism, 'Mouse is a monosyllable, a mouse eats

cheese, therefore a monosyllable eats cheese.' All these jokes illustrate the humour of language and misunderstanding. They are jokes about the use and misuse of words.

While these four main categories exist, a little thought must soon convince us that there is a sense in which all four categories are one and the same. Analyse them and it becomes apparent that each is a variation on the one theme: the contrast between what ought to be and what is. That is the central concept but it is based, in turn, on two other ideas. The first is the sense of proportion and the other is the sense of authority. Proportion is the relationship between the parts and the whole. It was a Greek discovery and they called it the Golden Mean. It is said that it was established by handing a stick to a number of people, saying 'Divide it unequally'. The average of the choices made thus represented the generally acceptable ratio between the part and the whole. Whatever their method may have been, they established their ideal as the ratio of root 5 minus 1 to 2, a proportion which has remained vital to good architecture from their day to ours.

In proportion, the Greeks saw the secret of bodily perfection, of beauty, of art and good behaviour. Disproportion, the wrong ratio or the excessive size, was one target, therefore, for their sense of humour. This joke is still in use on the stage, as when a small man with a big hat appears alongside a large man in a small hat. As important, however, was their sense of authority, which was itself governed by their sense of proportion. Their great men were important but were not imperial. If the ruler of Japan or Siam were to trip over the doormat it would be a serious matter, an evil omen, a disaster in itself and no occasion for mirth. Given a society in which all are equal—to take the opposite extreme—the mishap on the threshold would not be particularly funny. The joke depends upon the chief being respected but not worshipped; a descendant perhaps of the gods but not himself a manifestation of the deity. But our respect for the rulers of our society must also extend to the laws and customs, the manners and etiquette by which authority is normally surrounded. Here again proportion is vital. If the penalty for a breach of etiquette is death, the rule is more than a subject for laughter. If the point of etiquette is generally ignored its breach will not be amusing. The joke centres upon the rule which is generally upheld but not under penalty of death. The penalty for infringement is to become a target for mirth.

The tradition of British humour is based firmly upon the occasional flouting of an accepted authority. Old volumes of *Punch* are full of jokes about the social blunders of the newly-rich, the mistakes of ignorance in the hunting field, at Ascot or Henley. The humour of the Gilbert and Sullivan operas is very similarly based. In *Iolanthe* great fun is made of the House of Lords, the robed peers coming on the stage to explain their importance or lack of it. The joke succeeded before an audience to which the peerage seemed venerable. Part of the joke in *H.M.S. Pinafore* concerns a First Lord of the Admiralty who is totally ignorant of the sea. Here again the audience could be assumed to regard the Royal Navy as the cornerstone of British power, prosperity and influence. In *The Pirates of Penzance* there are equivalent jokes about the Army and the Police Force. In *Trial by Jury* the joke is similarly against the process of law. In these and other instances the authority accepted without question is held up to ridicule. No essential damage is done and people who might incline to be pompous are made, in effect, to laugh at themselves. The story is told of a great diplomatist that he had a technique for dealing with younger colleagues who would bustle into his room in too portentous a way. As the young man left, the great man would say, 'Remember Rule Six'. To this the reply would be, 'Yes, sir. Of course, sir'. At the door the young official would pause and turn back, asking, 'Excuse me, sir—but what is Rule Six?' The conversation then continued as follows:

'Rule six is "Don't take yourself too seriously".'

'Yes, sir. Thank you, sir. . . . But what are the other rules?'

'There are no other rules.'

Jokes against those in authority used to centre very largely upon the Army, the Navy and the Church. From World War I dates the classic picture of the squad being drilled by a newly-commissioned subaltern on the cliffs of Dover. The men are marching towards the cliff edge and the dithering young officer fails to remember any suitable word of command. Says the sergeant, helpfully, 'Say something, sir, if it's only goodbye.' From the same period we have the famous picture by H. M. Bateman of the guardsman who dropped his rifle. Many naval stories concern the use of signals. One, from World War II, centres upon a destroyer which, entering the fleet anchorage, fouled the anti-submarine netting, collided with a supply vessel, bounced off a tug and finally dropped anchor in the area reserved for aircraft carriers. Everyone looked to the flagship wondering what the reaction would be. When the signal came, flashed by a very visible searchlight, it consisted of one word, 'Good.' After a pause which seemed like eternity the signal was completed by the further word 'God'. There is an R.A.F. equivalent to that story and it tells of a German bomber on a mission over Britain which became detached from its formation, lost all sense of its whereabouts and finally landed on an airfield in Wiltshire, having mistaken the Bristol for the English Channel. Quitting their aircraft, the German crew started walking toward the control tower. At this juncture some sixth sense told the pilot that all was not well. It could have been a glimpse, perhaps, of the British flag. At any rate, he changed his mind and led his crew back to their 'plane. Starting the engine up, he taxied, took off and finally returned to base. An account of this incident went to all R.A.F. stations with the Air Ministry comment, 'This is unsatisfactory'. One feels even now that the Ministry had a point.

Jokes about the Church go back to the story of the curate's egg. The *Punch* drawing shows a nervous, chinless nincompoop of a curate who is having breakfast at the bishop's table. The curate's egg is rotten and the bishop, a formidable person, looks across at his hesitating guest and asks, 'Is your egg alright, Mr. Green?' or words to that effect. He is answered by the classic reply, 'Parts of it, my lord, are excellent.' Another episcopal joke concerns the bishop who is staying at a hotel. The servants were all instructed before-hand on the correct way of addressing a bishop and particular care was taken with the pageboy whose duty it would be to bring the bishop's boots into his lordship's bedroom. He was told to knock on the door and when the bishop should ask, 'Who is that?' he should answer, 'It's the boy, my lord.' When his big moment came, however, the pageboy was too confused to remember his lesson. 'It's the lord, my boy,' was his unauthorized version, and the bishop hid under the bed.

As for Archbishops, the best story tells how the Archbishop of Canterbury complained to the Prime Minister—Mr. Winston Churchill—about the insufficiency of his income. 'There is the upkeep, you see, of Lambeth Palace—a vast building. Do you realize, Prime Minister, that the palace has *forty* bedrooms?' 'Indeed?' said Winston, 'And I suppose there are only thirty-nine articles?' The ecclesiastical joke on an even higher level might be exemplified by a schoolboy howler. Asked 'What is a Papal Bull?', the boy answered, 'A cow kept in the Vatican to provide milk for the Pope's children.' Taking the joke even higher, we have the story of the boy who could find nothing to say about *any* examina-tion question. He finally scrawled across the answer book. 'God knows—I don't,' and then added (as it was December) 'Merry Christmas'. His papers came back marked, 'God passed—*you* didn't,' and then, 'Happy New Year.'

All these jokes, whether good or bad, pre-suppose a real respect for the institution concerned. They are rooted in a society in which ministers, peers, generals, admirals and bishops are august and formidable people. The joke about the curate's egg is meaningless unless the bishop is terrifying and the curate terrified. For all these jokes we need the background of a stable society, a sense of authority and a sense of proportion. The Homeric or primary joke implies that the chief is a person of real importance, respected but not deified. The joke about disappointment pre-supposes that most events take place as planned. In a country so inefficient that nothing takes place at the proper hour and in the proper place no joke is possible on the contrast between what we expect and what we find. In the same way the joke about sex is only funny in a society blessed with a norm from which deviation is possible. If there are no rules there can be nothing funny about their occasional infringement. As for the fourth joke, which is purely verbal, this pre-supposes a high level of education in the audience. In *The Rivals*, Sheridan has fun with Mrs. Malaprop, who uses long words without knowing what they mean. The scenes in which she appears can be mildly funny but only to people with a good vocabulary. This is a difficult age for the humorist because the needed background of sanity is going or has gone. Humour depends for its effect upon the very things we have chosen to discard, on the hierarchy we have abolished, on the discipline we no longer maintain, upon the institutions in which we no longer believe and the language of which we have forgotten the grammar and spelling. The comic actor has always needed his straight man or foil, the character who represents a sane normality. When this background of sanity has disappeared the funny man's jokes must cease to amuse. The essence of the joke lies, as we have seen, in the contrast between what ought to be and what is. As we discard conventions, restraints and rules of behaviour we find that we have also discarded humour. Lunacy and inconsequence remain but are meaningless without their opposites.

A chapter on humour can be serious indeed, no laughing matter at all. It is arguable, however, that it should at least end with a funny story. One possibility would be the tale of the American investor who noticed a certain share quoted at one nominal cent. Feeling that what cannot fall may possibly rise, he bought these shares to the value of ten thousand dollars. A day or two later he saw that his faith had been apparently justified. The shares now stood at two cents! He decided, therefore, to follow up his success. Having bought more shares, to the value again of ten thousand dollars, he watched eagerly to see how the market would respond. Again he proved right, the shares being now quoted at three cents. The wise speculator knows when the time has come to take a profit, and for him that moment had clearly come. Grabbing the telephone, he made contact with his broker, named the share and added the dramatic order: 'Sell!' From the other end of the line came his broker's weary reply, 'To *whom?*'

CHAPTER 12

On Genius

Honesty and ability are normally enough to ensure success in business, if combined with loyalty, energy and tact, but we hear from time to time of an altogether exceptional industrialist or merchant; one who is acclaimed, in fact, as a genius. It often transpires that the genius in industry is really an inventor or engineer, a Brunel or Marconi, and it cannot be said of such a man that business was ever his chief concern. There remain instances, however, of genius applied to business, as for example by Lorenzo de Medici or Thomas Gresham. While more everyday talents will serve most purposes in commerce, we know, therefore, that there is scope for genius when genius can be found. But is genius always given that scope? When we are confronted with a seemingly impossible task we tend nowadays to form a committee or appoint, at best, a man of experience and repute. But that sort of problem will be solved, if at all, by a stroke of genius. It is the more necessary, therefore, that we recognize genius when we see it. There is all too little available and what there is should be applied, surely, to the tasks for which genius is needed. Of all types of waste in a shockingly wasteful world, the waste of such talents as amount to genius must be thought the worst of all. It is the result, in part, of panic among the mediocre and in part through our failure to identify such genius as there may be available.

If we are to reduce wastage in this small but precious field we must answer one question at the outset. What is genius? Failing an answer to that our quest is in vain. We say, surely, that a man (or woman) has genius who combines outstanding ability with vision. But what, in that case, is ability and how is it distinguished from skill? A man has skill, we must all agree, when he does something which others would find difficult. He plays the cello, for example, repairs the television set, mends the car or writes a leading article for a well-known newspaper. He has ability, by contrast, when he deploys the skill of others, as in conducting an orchestra, organizing a garage or editing a magazine. Some people are abler than others and outstanding ability is shown by those who do better what many other people do well. A skilful man is often unable to explain what he does, but a man of ability is nearly always a good teacher, a man known for his success in making a difficult subject seem easy. Under an organizer and teacher of outstanding ability, each member of the team will know exactly what he is to do and when, how and why. The acid test of ability is the willingness and capacity to explain. Confidence is created and success is the result.

The man of ability makes good use of all that he is given; the situation, the people, the circumstances and material. Working with people and things he can understand, he produces the right answer to each problem as it arises. The producer of an opera is given a certain theatre and has to assemble there the carpenters, scene-painters and electricians. He collects the cast and conducts the rehearsals, co-ordinating the work of stage-manager, conductor, costume-designer and prompter. The views and efforts of many people have somehow to be reconciled, the great work reaching its culmination when the curtain rises on the first night. The success achieved must be the result of determination, persistence, experience, energy and tact. The producer has begun with a script, a musical score, an array of talent and a suitable stage, the final result being the opera as performed. That the producer has artistic talent is highly probable but the achievement we have first to applaud is his assembly of the right talents at the right place on the right day. His task has been, first and foremost, one of organization. We see the same sort of abilities at work in planning an exhibition, staging a conference, directing a pageant or arranging a public funeral. The elements of each occasion are in existence and the problem of direction is one of assembly and sequence, placing and timing, deployment and dispersal. Whoever is to direct must be very able indeed.

In complete contrast with ability is vision. A man or woman of vision is able to imagine what cannot be seen and may not even exist. He forms a mental picture of the thing imagined—a clear, vivid and precise image. It could be something evil but it is more often something ideal—a city, a symphony, an invention, a utopia. The vision is distant and seemingly unattainable and the problem, for the visionary, is to find a way back from his vision to where he actually is. The acid test of vision is the *inability*—not the reluctance—to explain. A vision cannot be described or analysed. Knowing that she was right, Joan of Arc could only convey her ideas by saying that an angel had appeared to her and told her what to do next. Between the person of ability and the person of vision there is the same sort of difference which exists between the research worker and the inventor. The research worker starts from where someone else has left off. Given certain facts and certain accepted theories, he feels for the next rung on the ladder which leads upwards to he knows not what. The good scientist is content to take one step at a time. The inventor has a vision of the finished work and then tries to find his way back to the point where he actually stands. In theory, great things might be accomplished by the collaboration of ability with vision. In practice it is seldom possible for people to work together whose mental processes are so unlike. The practical man and the eccentric dreamer remain far apart. One may work to death and the other may starve to death. Neither is a genius and one of them may be mad.

The genius is the man or woman in whom these two opposite qualities are somehow and surprisingly combined. He has both the vision which defines the aim and the ouststanding ability which suggests the means. The path traced onward from where he is joins up with the path traced backwards from where he wants to go. That is genius, a quality shared by Abraham Lincoln and Walt Disney. In either we can recognize that dreamy attitude, that hint of poetry and humour which we might associate with failure. In each we can also recognize the practical shrewdness which led to success. There are instances in which a national emergency has added the gift of vision to someone whose outstanding ability had long been recognized. There are other instances of the dreamer who suddenly finds his feet in politics, commerce or war. There are some who believe that the triumphs of tomorrow will be the result of teamwork, not of genius. There are scientific fields in which this may be true but there are other areas—including the industrial and the commercial—in which nothing would seem less probable. In these, as in art and music, as in literature and drama, we can be sure that the greatest of achievements are reserved for the greatest of men.

If we want more genius it is reasonable to ask how the supply can be improved. Genius cannot be trained and it is far from clear that it can even be bred. All that we can do is to increase the arithmetical chances of genius appearing while resolving, at the same time, not to waste it when it appears. How are these chances to be increased? To improve the chances of some outstandingly able man having vision, or of some dreamer revealing practical ability, we need to have the largest number of each. But opposite conditions must be needed for producing opposite results. To produce a high level of ability, above which some abilities will appear outstanding, there must be a certain stability. To encourage vision there should be, ideally, both stimulus and conflict. That being so, we might guess that societies most productive of genius are those which combine a divergence of ideas with a general agreement on the standards of accomplishment. Such a society was Elizabethan England, the background for the genius of William Shakespeare and Francis Drake—each a good example of outstanding ability combined with vision. The ability of each rose above a high average achievement. Shakespeare's supremacy was thus established over a generation of men who wrote both verse and prose with great distinction. Drake's supremacy was established over a generation of men who combined enterprise with perseverance and skill. But the world in which men could agree on the merits of blank verse and gunnery, navigation and madrigals, was one in which they could agree, it would seem, on very little else.

It would be wrong, however, to overstress this contrast between the accepted standards of technical achievement and the current dissensions about basic belief. There is something of this same contrast to be seen, it is true, in the lives of Peter Abelard, Joan of Arc, Erasmus, Leonardo da Vinci, Isaac Newton, Johann Sebastian Bach, Mozart, Nelson, Darwin, Lincoln, Einstein and Gandhi. It might, however, be difficult to prove that the absence of dissension would have meant, in every case, the absence of genius. During centuries of conflict there can be no background—whether for genius or stupidity—other than the conflicts which exist. What one would rather emphasize, as perhaps less open to dispute, is the other aspect: that high level of average achievement upon which the work of genius is usually (if not invariably) based. For, granted that dissensions may be stimulating, and that their absence (as for centuries in China) may produce a dull conformity, we have still stronger reason for thinking that a genius often stands, in effect, upon the shoulders of other men.

To illustrate this concept of a high level of achievement, from which genius can spring still higher, here are some examples of Elizabethan prose:

For myself, if I have in anything served my country and prized it before my private [interest], the general acceptance can yield me no other profit at this time, than doth a fair sunshine day to a seaman after shipwreck, and the contrary, no other harm than an outrageous tempest after the port attained.

A genius often stands, in effect, upon the shoulders of other men

To the same first ages do belong the report of many inventions therein found, and from them derived to us; though most of the authors' names have perished in so long a navigation. For those ages had their laws; they had kingly rule, nobility, policy in war, navigation, and all or most of the needfull trades . . .

. . . . it is certain, let us claw the reader with never so many courteous phrases, yet shall we evermore be thought fools that write foolishly.

. . . Certainly there is no other account to be made of this ridiculous world, than to resolve that the change of fortune on the great theatre is but as the change of garment on the less . . .

. . . . But let every man value his own wisdom, as he pleaseth. Let the rich man think all fools that cannot equal his abundance; the revenger esteem all negligent that have not trodden down their opposites:—the politician all gross that cannot merchandise their faith; yet, when we once come in sight of the port of death, to which all winds drive us, and when, by letting fall that fatal anchor, which can never be weighed again, the navigation of this life takes end; then it is, I say, that our cogitations (those sad and severe cogitations, formerly beaten from us by our health and felicity) return again, and pay us to the uttermost for all the pleasing passages of our lives past . . . it is only then, that we are struck through the soul with the terrible sentence, *That God will not be mocked.*

. . . . It is therefore Death alone that can suddenly make man to know himself. He tells the proud and insolent that they are but abjects, and humbles them at the instant; makes them cry, complain and repent; yea, even to hate their forepast happiness. He takes the account of the rich, and proves him a beggar . . . He holds a glass before the eyes of the most beautiful, and makes them see therein their deformity and rottenness; and they acknowledge it.

O eloquent, just and mighty Death! Whom none could advise, thou hast persuaded; what none hath dared, thou has done; and whom all the world hath flattered, thou hast cast out of the world and despised:—thou hast drawn together all the far stretched greatness, all the pride, cruelty and ambition of man, and covered it all over with these two narrow words— *Hic jacet.*

One not too versed in Elizabethan literature might attribute the first passage, about storm and shipwreck, to Sir Francis Drake; the second and third to Sir Francis Bacon; the fourth, about the theatre, to Shakespeare (echoing his passage about all the world being a stage), the fifth to some Elizabethan bishop; and the sixth, correctly, to Sir Walter Raleigh, whose famous passage on death— written by a prisoner under a capital sentence—must be well known to all. In fact, *all* these quotations come from Sir Walter Raleigh's *History of the World*. Raleigh was not among the first seamen of his day. He was only moderately successful as a politician and only mildly distinguished as an author. His works today are read by nobody. And yet we can judge for ourselves that he could write. Dare any of us claim, indeed, to write so well? It is evident, surely, that Shakespeare had a high standard to surpass.

Take another example, this time in verse.

Who seekes by worthie deedes to gain renowne for hire,
Whose hart, whose hand, whose purse is prest to purchase
    his desire,
If anie such there be, that thirsteth after fame,
Lo, heare a meane, to winne himself an everlasting name.

One might think this not as good, although still competent. The author, in this case, is Sir Francis Drake, whose only education was acquired on board ship.

Turn now to the greatest, in some ways, of the Elizabethans; Queen Elizabeth herself. How does she rank as a writer of prose?

Jesus: what availeth wit when it fails the owner at greatest need? Do that you are bidden, and leave your considerations for your own affairs: for in some things you had clear commandment, which you did not; and in others none, and did; yea, to the use of those speeches from me that might oblige me to more than I was bound or mind ever to yield. We Princes be wary enough of our bargains . . . I am assured of your dutiful thought, but I am utterly at squares with this childish dealing.

How did she express herself at the crisis of her reign, when the Spanish Armada was on the English coast?

You may assure yourself that, for my part, I doubt no whit but that all this tyrannical, proud and brainsick attempt will be the beginning, though not the end, of the ruin of that King, that, most unkingly, even in the midst of treating peace, begins this wrongful war. He hath procured my greatest glory that meant my sorest wrack, and hath so dimmed the light of his sunshine, that who hath a will to obtain shame, let them keep his forces company.

Here is the wording of the reproof she sent to Henri IV of France, whose cause she was supporting:

From our enemies we were expecting nothing but every evil dealing, and our friends lend us as much; what difference do we find? I am astonished that any one, who is so much beholden to us for aid in his need, should pay his most assured friend in such base coin. Can you imagine that the softness of my sex deprives me of the courage to resent a public affront? The royal blood I boast could not brook, from the mightiest Prince in Christendom, such treatment as you have within the last three months offered to me. Be not displeased if I tell you roundly, that if thus you treat your friends . . . they will fail you hereafter at your greatest need.

Under a Queen who could write as eloquently as this there were many of her subjects who could express themselves in prose or verse. There were many notable captains on land and at sea. Among the writers of today there are few who can write as well as did the Elizabethans whose reputation had been gained with the sword. Not all of us, for that matter, could boast the military record of some Elizabethans whose fame had been achieved with the pen. That is why the best of all in that age needed not ability but genius.

Many must be good before one can be supreme. Suppose we can today produce a hundred extremely able industrialists and as many composers, civil engineers and novelists, there is some chance of genius being found among them. But if we could produce a *thousand* extremely able lawyers or painters, the chances would be ten times as great. In practice, moreover, the chances would be better than that, for the competition would be tense, and it is rivalry which brings out that final burst of activity; the effort which carries genius to a greater height than ability can reach.

Reference has been made to a high plateau of achievement, and that term is used deliberately; for a total effort too dispersed will never form the platform from which genius can spring. To be the best composer in a tiny group of like-minded musicians is easy. To be the most eccentric architect in a small coterie of eccentric architects is no great feat. To be first among the Islington school of artists, that select group of abstract non-existentialists whose works are executed in cottonwool, gravel, brass wire and icing sugar (supposing such a group exists) is not especially difficult. To be the most obscure among a school of poets famous for their obscurity is not, in itself, a valid claim to rank among the immortals. And what if you are the only designer of a museum built like a corkscrew? It is the best of its kind. It is also the worst and indeed the average. What if you are the only contractor who builds in nothing but coloured glass? How if your writing is beyond the comprehension of all but your closest disciples? The result in each case is that you lack the competition from which excellence can result. Success is too easy when the field is too small.

In the development of genius, then, a vital part is played by the rest of us. It is for us to keep the average high. Should it fall through our failure to make an effort, the average will be too easy to excel. Those above the average will have won their place too cheaply and can afford to take things easily. It is those who run them close who prevent this and can share the credit for the final success. The athletic record is broken on the day when competition is fierce, and is broken most likely by the representative of the largest and most enthusiastic club. It is the same in business or politics, in drama or art. It is only when many are good that one will emerge as supreme. It is that one man or woman we want and no number of the mediocre will do instead. We have no means of producing genius save by providing a high plateau of achievement. That done, our further task is to recognize genius when we see it. This book begins with a description of the fur-lined mousetrap, the economic predicament into which our society has drifted. If there is a way out of the trap it will be for a genius to find it. Towards finding that genius this last chapter is a humble contribution. If it does not solve the problem it may do something, at least, to point the way.